A Young Innovator's Guide to PLANNING FOR SUCCESS

Developing an Authentic Personal Narrative
for Students, Educators, and Parents

GITANJALI RAO

Post Hill
PRESS

A POST HILL PRESS BOOK
ISBN: 979-8-88845-274-5
ISBN (eBook): 979-8-88845-275-2

A Young Innovator's Guide to Planning for Success:
Developing an Authentic Personal Narrative for Students, Educators, and Parents

Cover design by Conroy Accord

Post Hill Press
New York • Nashville
posthillpress.com

Published in the United States of America
1 2 3 4 5 6 7 8 9 10

Also by Gitanjali Rao

A Young Innovator's Guide to STEM:
5 Steps to Problem Solving for Students, Educators, and Parents

I dedicate this book to...
All my mentors who believed in me
and allowed me to fail and learn.
All my teachers and counselors for being my
tireless guides in my journey of learning.
All the organizations that invested in me,
hoping for a better future for all of us.
My parents, grandparents, and younger brother
for their constant support and patience.

CONTENTS

WELCOME

For the last two to three years, as I met thousands of students, there were several questions related to academics—my scores, my grades, my college choices, my extracurriculars, my summer programs, and many more.

These were very real unknowns for me and many students as we planned our high school years.

I have received multiple viewpoints: hundreds of videos on my chances of going to a top ten school, much advice on what I should or should not take up as extracurriculars, and a cookie cutter plan from several high-end college counselors who decided the best way to get to the top schools. I am sure so many students go through this, and there are many of us who are not given any major guidance but are still expected to find all of this ourselves and stumble through a college application process.

When I conducted workshops or had a chance to speak to high school students I commonly received several questions from students who were anxious of what next after high school:

- How many Advance Placement (AP) classes should I take?

- I received a B. Did I miss my chance of getting into my dream school?

- How do you get into pre-collegiate summer programs?

- Some of the summer programs at top Ivy schools can cost up to $8,000 and I can't afford that. What should I do?

- Were you part of Math, Bio, Chem and other olympiads? Is it necessary to get in to the Top 10?

- Reddit and some college sites show that a student with my stats didn't get into his/her dream school. What should I do?

- Can you tell me all your AP classes and their scores!

- What is your GPA and if I aim for it, will I get in the college of my choice?

- How did you highlight your achievements in your essays? Can I get your essays and try the same next year?

- Did you get SAT/ACT tutors?

- Why are you continuing with vocal lessons when that is not going to improve your college profile?

- Why are you still applying to science fairs if you are the *TIME* Kid of the Year?

- My parents are not discussing financials with me. How will I know if they will pay for the college of my choice?

- In the International Science Engineering Fair, some students even went to the extent of hiring a coach to scan their project and share weaknesses/strengths so that they could have a fair chance. I don't have that kind of money to do this! What are my options?

- How much did you pay to create a website of your own and whom should I contact? I was told we need to do this between the summer of junior and senior.

- How to create my professional profile on LinkedIn in order to increase my chances of getting accepted?

- Why are you still involved in conducting workshops and community service, when college acceptance season is done?

Is it easy to get research opportunities? Where do I start? Does it help to know somebody in prestigious schools like Harvard and Stanford?

Some of these questions were eye-openers during my journey. For example, I didn't know people hired professional coaches to go through science fairs, publish papers, and create extracurricular websites during the last month before applications were due in a race to show our differentiation in the college applications. While there are many of us who are completely oblivious to this process and go through our normal high school plans and try our best with what is provided within the school and outside the community, there are countless students who are exposed to this practice and believe they get the advantage.

There were lots of other questions like these, but you get the general idea. Many of them wanted me to write down how I went through the last four years in high school and why I am still continuing my work when I've already been accepted to college. How did I face the extracurricular drama of college applications and competitions in and out of school? How did my friends at school feel when someone got an early acceptance? Is every part of my profile needed for acceptances?

I decided to write this book, my second one, *A Young Innovator's Guide to Planning for Success*, to answer many of these questions. Coming from someone roughly their own age, I hope the book will help millions of teenagers manage themselves and plan their own high school journey without fearing the competition around them, spending hours to monitor and create a profile similar to other successful students or fearing the rejection and acceptance letters at the end of their high school experience.

The book aims to highlight the open conversations teens should have with their parents, a perspective from parents on how they should support their teen, areas I believe schools can help with, relationships that are important, and lastly a personal academic plan and extracurriculars that help to grow up as responsible adults who give back to the community. The book also provides some academic plan templates that may help you plan your entire high school academics.

Best of luck in your journey and remember college acceptances are just the start of your journey!

INTRODUCTION

Hello and welcome! Just by opening up this book, I can tell that you have the drive to help unfold your passion and ensure success within high school and even outside of it. I hope that I can truly bring that goal of yours to life. I wrote this book not as an exact special process on how to plan out high school and maintain the right mindset, but instead as a guide for how to navigate it. Many say that high school was some of the best years of their life, and while that may be true for some (and definitely not true for others), it's very easy to get caught up in the different elements that make up high school: academics, extracurriculars, social life, relationships, and so much more. This book outlines everything that I wish my high school self knew when jumping into it—so think of this as a personal note from me to you.

I have split this book into the five big pillars separated as sections that I believe made up high school for me and ones that I focused the most on to create the portfolio and application that I have today:

Passion/Purpose
Skills
Academics/Extracurriculars
Achievement
Leadership

I would suggest using a mnemonic to carry this with you. Here's the one that I use: "Pet Snails Are Always Lazy"—a great way to remember it, and a great reminder when buying a pet. Each of these individual pillars not only provides a great starting point, but is something to keep in mind through college, and even beyond. This is primarily for US universities; however, the pillars can be used by any students who have an ambition to study in the US. Now that we've learned a little bit about the components of this book, let's talk about how to read it and who it's for.

Who is This Book For?

In this book, we are going to go through a framework for high-school years that will help you connect your passion to courses and extracurriculars. The end goal is for you to find the best option to continue your education after high school while keeping alive your true passions and commitments. It is a great read for not just for middle school and high school students who are getting ready for college admissions, but parents, educators and counselors who can provide guidance on course plans, extracurriculars, admission process with plan templates and resources.

Students

You will have the chance to read through and plan your high school years rather than waiting till the last minute to figure out your career, developing a strong portfolio or trading off between courses and pursuing your passions. You will have an easy framework that will determine the skills you need to stick to your plan and that will help beyond your high school years. Feel free to use the empty templates to make it your own such as course placemat, transcript monitoring, portfolio example, recommendation requests, sample essays and plans.

Parents

You will have a book full of readymade plans and resources to guide your children through high school years and "Parent Notes," specifically called out in the book, that help see all perspectives. The high-level plan from freshman to senior years, includes the courses and the recommended number of courses, for example AP courses, that make it optimal and manageable. The book provides samples of extracurriculars that you can guide them including reasons for building an organization. The book also includes pitfalls at every stage that we teenagers can stumble into, so you can support us. This book allows you to ask the right questions to your school counselors along with your student to understand the academic rigor needed for your child. I hope the samples I provided allows you and your children to not focus on the short-term, but the long-term plan for their success and growth.

Counselors/Educators

You have plan templates, course placemats and portfolio templates that you can directly assign to your students at the beginning of freshman year and guide them throughout the four years. This will enable your students to be on the driver seat for their journey while you can guide them. Well before the senior year, you will have an understanding of their motivations, passions, the right recommendations they need to request and their college of choice. The book provides samples and templates to engage and communicate well with the student and their parents/guardians while making it personalized for every student.

This book benefits ANYONE willing to support high school students and encourage them to be responsible adults while navigating the college admission process with confidence. I wanted to write this to involve every adult who are supporting high school students to make it an engaging experience so that you just don't remember just the high school year, but a memory of making it a fun and engaging experience for all students. While I found many books written by admission counselors and educational consultants on what to do in the years of high school to get to a Top Ivy League school, I hardly found books written by students my age, who told me the practical steps to go about it with personal experiences on both the ups and downs we all go through those years. There are millions of videos on "how to" and their portfolio of successful students, which I found useful, but blank templates with plans and examples would have been more efficient for me as I embarked my high school journey.

How to Read This Book?

The nice thing about this book is that there's no correct way to read it. When I was originally writing it, I chose to write parts of it that applied to me the most at that point in time. Therefore, if you believe you'd benefit from learning more about course planning or maintaining a positive mindset, or just hopping throughout and taking bits and pieces from each chapter, feel free to do that! However, while you're navigating through this book, I'd suggest keeping an eye out for a couple of icons:

When you see this icon, that means this is an important tip to remember or an added detail that I believe can help you through your process of perfecting high school!

When you see this icon, this is a downloadable worksheet or link that you can access to get some more hands-on experience with planning and setting yourself up for success.

When you see this icon, this is a note that my parents have taken the time to write to help educate other parents who may be reading this book to ease them through the process and help them understand that they are not alone!

Take this journey slow. Your high school years aren't supposed to be stressful; they should be an opportunity for you to learn and grow and thrive. This book is made for you to explore everything and everyone around you. The only person you need to compare yourself is your previous you and how much you can improve. I can guarantee you will take away something!

CHAPTER 1

Framework for Success

Timing: Through Your High School Years

The purpose of planning your high school years is not just to get into a dream college but to shape your future equipped with soft skills and academic skills that will help you choose a career and be a responsible adult. The college admission process has added so much stress, competition, self-esteem issues, guilt, and mental health issues to the extent that the impact on we teenagers are ignored. The focus is on grades and scores and showing extracurriculars that do not make sense to us. Our grades, scores, and awards do not define us. The race to start nonprofits without purpose and to call ourselves the founders, CEOs, and leaders does not define us. College acceptance and rejection letters do not define us.

Our passion, purpose, what we enjoy, our attitude towards learning, and what we want to do defines us. Therefore, to make it easier on all of us, I came up with a framework that we can adhere to as closely as possible and be authentic to who we are. There are college counselors, parents, teachers, and expensive admission counselors who provide insight into what makes a great college essay and an application. But the person who defines us is ourselves, whether we are quirky, confident, introverted, extroverted, socially awkward, or have other characteristics.

Below is a framework I decided to base my high school experience around. I saw each one feeding the one above it; I repurposed it from Maslow's Hierarchy of Needs pyramid, which was introduced to me in middle school. Let's call it a Pyramid of Purpose with an acronym that may be easy for all of us to remember.

"Pet Snails Are Always Lazy"

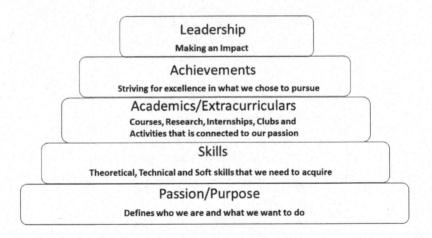

Passion/Purpose

The foundation has to have a purpose and passion. We are not defined by our grades and scores but as an individual who loves art, music, writing, food, building, sports, history, science, math, and more. We do certain things because we enjoy it. This can be different for different students. All STEM majors need not program, and not all engineers need to build. All musicians don't have to be in the school band, and all athletic students don't need to be varsity players. If you follow your passion with a purpose, we will be unstoppable in what we can achieve.

Skills

We need to gain skills to develop our passion and purpose. No one is born a genius, and no one is born with an inborn talent. We may all have some basic inclination, but it takes years to develop and excel in it. As the saying goes, "Practice makes us perfect." Skills can be academic—such as programming, research, science, coding, math, and history—or non-academic skills—such as art, music, and communication (written, athletic, or spoken). In the chapters on skills, I have added some basic skills we all need to have, no matter our passion, including time management, a positive mindset, communication, and handling relationships.

Academics/Extracurriculars

To develop the skills, you must find experiences with extracurriculars and academic courses. Courses must align with your extracurriculars and passion while making you well-rounded. Depending on your passion, it could be research, an internship in an organization that aligns with your interest, activities, and clubs in your school that will help you develop the skills.

Achievements

Your skills will help you develop excellence in the area you are passionate about. Aim for excellence in the area. This could mean applying for contests and challenges, refining your skills, competing at different levels, measuring yourself, and improving further.

Leadership

Finally, use your talent and excellence achieved to impact others. Impacts do not mean starting a nonprofit organization and calling yourself a leader. Impact means to give back to society meaningfully. It could be using your talent to provide value and make a difference for others. For example, you could be good at writing, so you can find venues to write articles to bring awareness to a societal issue, or you could be a musician and write songs or perform in assisted living centers and nursing homes to make a difference for them. Find a fit between leadership and your passion, which will then seem like something other than work but will be a way of life to give back beyond college applications.

Each can be adapted to your likes and dislikes. There is no set way to pick the activities or academics, and every student is unique. Be a pioneer in what you do and continue being part of the activities you chose!

PASSION/PURPOSE

*"All our dreams can come true if we
have the courage to pursue them."*

—WALT DISNEY

Description: *The following chapter will provide you some insights
into what passion truly means. The goal is to help you define your
passion as something you could wake up and miss doing and
demonstrate that effectively within high school and while writing
your college applications. Don't shy away from who you are, that's
what people want to hear!*

CHAPTER 2

High School Planning

Timing: Through High School Years

How do you define your passion and purpose? This is a common question that I was asked during high school. How do you manage to do all the things that you do while also managing your high school workload? My activities had a central theme, and each was an interconnected extension of the other. While it may look to the outside world that I have nine different things going on and may not have the time, it was all related to a central passion for problem-solving and sharing what I learned as a process or framework with others.

Here are a few steps that helped me, and you can try them out for yourself:

Step 1: Find What Inspires You

First, we need to understand what we love to do most and what inspires us. This can be anything—art, music, writing, reading about history, theater, cooking, speaking, solving, or something else.

Liking a subject is not passion! Doing something with a purpose is passion.

If you are unable to define it yourselves, request your teachers', friends', mentors', or parents' help. You could ask them questions on what you genuinely enjoy doing. They may have seen you from a different perspective than you have seen yourself. For example, I genuinely like teaching and explaining, and I want to be understood. My parents noticed that I would quickly learn a subject and help my teachers teach the class or help a student. It didn't matter to me what I taught. All it mattered to me was I explained something in a way that the person in front of me understood.

Step 2: Choose Skills/Subjects/Activities That Easily Relate To

Find something that comes natural to you, something that needs very little effort and doesn't feel like work. We all innately have something that we feel comes easy to us. This could be coding, art, acting, sports, or anything else. It doesn't have to be one. It could be multiple talents. You may be an expert in a subject, and your friends come to you for help or an opinion. Try an activity with a purpose in that subject to see if you enjoy it. Go for it with no fear of failure. There may be a local art club, flying club, or something you always feared to be part of because you may not be good at it. Try that out! This is the time to try that. I always wanted to try building a cookie bridge and try my engineering skills. I did that in my freshman year with a team, and it was a disaster! I learned to bake better later and liked it, but I decided against my architectural career to design buildings and bridges.

I noticed that my ability to come up with a solution, no matter how impossible, came naturally to me. I would devise ideas that made no sense to anyone I spoke to. I would go into a restaurant and dream of tables/chairs underground and popping up like in science fiction movies to make it more interesting for the customers and also save space for the long-term problem of overcrowding.

No matter what it was, I had to come up with some ideas, and it was non-stop! Every idea of mine was to do something automatically and magically with machines and technologies.

Step 3: Connect Your Inspiration and Skills

Now try to combine what you enjoy and your strengths. It may feel difficult, but there is always a way! You love to write, and science is natural to you. You love history, and theater/acting is also something you enjoy. You may love teaching, and cooking is also your passion. You may love hearing music, and also relate to math. It can be any combination! It doesn't have to be something where there is a lucrative career or something you are forced to like because you're at a STEM school. Think of all the ways you can put both of these together.

Science/technology, problem-solving, music, and teaching seemed to come together for me.

Step 4: Identify One Principle That You Will Adhere to When You Follow the Passion

I love Sean Covey's book, *The 7 Habits of Highly Effective Teens*, and one idea that stuck with me was his message to pick a principle. This could be commitment, persistence, integrity, quality work, diligence, or some other meaningful principle. This is the most important step in building a roadmap. It is very easy to move away from our passion, purpose, plan, and goal if we don't consistently adhere to one principle. I chose commitment. No matter the pressure of scores, grades, homework, time, and social activities, if I committed to doing something I will fulfill it.

Step 5: Define Who Can Use Your Passion or Talent and How You Can Help Them

Use your talent to see if there is a need in the local community. A win-win exists since we can strengthen our talent and benefit others. Examples could be you like to read and can do that for children in the library; you like art and can help students and elderly learn crafts in local assisted centers. You may love music and play an instrument. You can use your musical talent in local assisted living centers and hospitals. I did this for years in Nashville when I was in middle school, and many students started following the path into high school. Use kindness and empathy as the central theme. Do not expect anything back from others. Just figure out what you would enjoy giving to society, your community, or your school. Have fun with it as much as you can.

Make this your purpose for your high school years.

You can write it down in bold: "I will use my talent to help the local community or my school."

Step 6: Accept Help to See If There Is a Career Path with the Outputs of Steps 1 to 5

You love to write, but also are passionate about science. Can you start a science blog? Can you write articles on scientific topics? Can you be a researcher, professor, science journalist, or entrepreneur?

You love history, and theater/acting is natural for you. Have you thought about writing plays that involve history or culture? How about plays with a historical theme? Maybe you can think about being a historian or archaeologist?

You love traveling and are an athletic person. Maybe professional athletics and traveling for sports might be a thing for you ?

Again, these are my thoughts, but I am sure you will come with many more than I came up with here—or you may not have to come with a career just yet. You can use this to explore your high school years and decide if this is a fit for you. Once you enroll in undergraduate studies, you can choose a different career path, but this is what you may feel like now!

Step 7: Put All This Together and Prepare to Jumpstart Your High School Years

It's okay if you have to repeat the above steps in your freshman or sophomore year.

Passion/Purpose Worksheet

Now that you have defined your passion, here is a path to follow: No matter what you define as a passion for yourself, show commitment to the activity and show that you have improved and excelled to the best of your ability. Finally, "lead" and give back to society. This skill will stay with you longer than college acceptances.

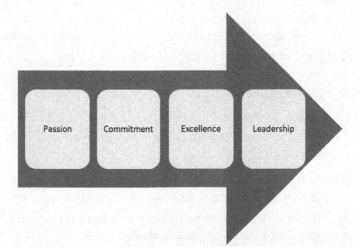

Passion → Commitment → Excellence → Leadership

Once you define your passion and purpose for what you enjoy and want to do long-term, create a roadmap for your four years. The roadmap for your high school years should follow a pattern of starting with your passions, being committed to them, getting excellent at them, and finally being a leader. Joining multiple clubs and doing hundreds of activities may waste your time if it's not connected to your passion and purpose.

Here is the general sequence of activities that may help you plan your four years:

Freshman Year

Academics: Focus on building a strong foundation in all subjects and maintaining a high GPA from the start. We will discuss course planning in a separate chapter.

Extracurricular Activities: Join school clubs or start clubs, and reach out to local sports teams or community service organizations that combine your passion and purpose. Start small! We will expand on this more in a later chapter: Selecting Extracurriculars.

Example: You may love to play piano. Enhance your instrument-playing skills and see ways to compete locally or in the state. Now, start playing piano in a local club. Find a fit between your passion and the service or activity.

Sophomore Year

Academics: Continue to challenge yourself with advanced courses. Seek help from teachers or tutors if needed to maintain your GPA.

Extracurricular Activities: Narrow down your interests and commit to a few activities that genuinely inspire you. Expand your activities to the ones you picked in freshman year if you enjoy them and start excelling at them.

Example: This could be getting others to join you in piano, facilitating events in the same local club, and expanding to other clubs.

Junior Year

Academics: Take the most challenging courses available to you. Excel in your classes, as junior-year grades are critical for college admissions. Admission officers like to see your growth as an individual, no matter the circumstance.

Standardized Tests: Begin test preparation for the SAT or ACT. Consider taking the PSAT to qualify for National Merit Scholarships. Find the scores you need to aim for your dream university, and focus on that as your goal.

Extracurricular Activities: Demonstrate deep involvement and leadership in your chosen extracurriculars. Quality over quantity is essential. Measure yourself and redefine achievable goals.

Tip on Starting Organizations: There is no pressure to start an organization or nonprofit if your dream school is one of the top ten. I did not start any organization since there were multiple organizations with the same goal that I could easily collaborate with. Starting and maintaining an organization might have mundane administrative tasks that take away your passion. It makes sense if the organization has a unique vision where funds are needed, and you have not found others in the area. Plus, you need to structure to expand your activity. There are hundreds of "Women in STEM" and "STEM" or "Coding" organizations that have been started in the last ten years. Your cycles, effort, and time to start would not be any unique measurement of your skills and leadership. Instead, your ability to collaborate would probably be a better measure; you can learn from these organizations and eventually find a way if there is a need to create your own.

Example: If we follow the piano theme, apply for awards and scholarships with your ability to expand your community service. Form an organization with a vision and mission of enhancing and providing opportunities to others with the network you formed. This will give you the motivation to expand your leadership.

Senior Year

Academics: Maintain your strong academic performance throughout your senior year. Personally, this was a tough one for me. With college applications, early acceptances, and wanting to enjoy my senior year, I could have been more consistent. There were ups and downs. Taking breaks and coming back to focus on academics is very important. Retrospectively, I did not choose the right courses here for my second term and could have picked the ones I genuinely enjoyed better. Remember this when you pick your second term courses in the senior year! Acceptances and rejections impact you and your mental state, no matter how strong you are, with your convictions that do not define you.

Extracurriculars: Continue your leadership roles, and make a positive impact in your community. Keep expanding on the same activities, or find a way to continue them in college. To do this, you can talk to the adults who provided you with opportunities, and discuss ways to keep it going beyond your schedule and location change.

Consider assigning leaders or recruiting volunteers so the activity continues and people still benefit from what you started.

Examples:
1. Formalize roles and allow others to lead facilitating events in the local clubs, maybe those in their junior year.
2. Find a way to facilitate events remotely, if you are not around.

3. Create a process such as volunteer sign-up sheets, calendars, events every month, and similar designs, so your schedule and location don't have to hinder continuing the impacts and benefits.

Standardized Tests: Take SAT/ACT tests as necessary, and submit your scores to colleges of interest. These may change in the future, but there will be some form of test for colleges to decide your aptitude.

Use collegevine.com to add your dream universities and your profile to see the right scores that may increase your chances of acceptance.

College Applications: Start early on your college applications, including writing compelling essays with the theme of your centralized passion and securing strong letters of recommendation.

Interviews: Prepare for college interviews if required by your chosen colleges.

Financial Aid and Scholarships: Research and apply for scholarships and financial aid options.

There are multiple scholarships that we can apply for. There are hundreds of websites that share the scholarship names, and this changes often. Therefore, I do not intend to spend time in this book mentioning the scholarship names and application process.

The following are some common ones to look for scholarships:

- collegeboard.org
- fastweb.com
- scholarships.com
- unigo.com
- studentscholarshipsearch.com

Positive Attitude and Being Kind: This is probably the most important thing to know. As teenagers, especially in the high school years, our self-esteem, self-worth, and ego can go through a rollercoaster ride. We need to empathize with our peers who are going through the same. Showing off your scores, grades, and college acceptances will not boost your ego. College acceptance does not define us. Empathize with others going through the journey, and deal with the acceptance and rejections just like how you dealt with competitions and contests in the past. Not everyone can win in the competitions. But we try, and sometimes we win, and sometimes we lose. College acceptances follow the same pattern. You may get into the college of your choice, or you may not. There are hundreds of other colleges; you can try the next one. Most importantly, do not put down others for your benefit. Everybody is trying and is on the same journey as you.

High School Planning Sheet

Now, let's see an example of three students and how they planned their high school roadmap:

Student 1 has a passion clearly indicated by the student's extracurriculars. The student showed commitment to the same activity, excelled, and used their knowledge to help other students in the community. The student started with low-challenging courses and followed a path to end with advanced courses, showing growth as an individual. This creates a clear portfolio with no gaps in what they have done over the years.

Student 2 just decided to join any and all activities as and when they wanted to. No clear passion was defined, and the focus was on a high GPA, no matter the level of classes or the focus of the career path. The student also wants to highlight achievements through several high-profile positions in all clubs. This is a typical profile of lot of high schoolers with unclear objectives but assume that having high scores and being part of lot of activities and club can show achivement.

Student 3 started on the right path with the right courses and the right number of activities. Still, the national recognitions, competitions, and wins put him/her on a path where extracurriculars took precedence over academics. The grades started to slide down at the peak time.

I have no qualms in stating that I have been Student 1, Student 2, and Student 3 many times in the last four years, only to realize that I need to focus on a goal beyond my four years of high school—which is to be ready for undergraduate and continue what I love to do. You may be a student reading this in junior year or senior year. If that is the case, you have to trace back and see a common theme of passion for yourself and stick to that in the future and remove any other activity you are just involved with for the sake of profile, title, or friends. In terms of academics, find out why your grades dropped if they did, and if there is a way to keep doing your best, which shows your resilience and tenacity to finish strong.

While in school, I continued my passion to contribute to the community, but stayed focused on skill sets I need to demonstrate in my applications and be ready for college.

Year	Activities	Student 1	Student 2	Student 3
Freshman	Academics and Grade	Low challenging courses 4.0 Unweighted	Medium challenging courses 4.0 Unweighted	High challenging courses 4.0 Unweighted
	Extracurriculars	One sport, school club (FBLA or DECA)	Three school clubs, two seasonal sports, NHS, Student Government	Internships, several clubs, National Winner in competitions
Sophomore	Academics and Grade	Low to medium challenging courses 4.0 Unweighted	Medium challenging courses to maintain GPA 4.0 Unweighted	High challenging courses 3.9 Unweighted
	Extracurriculars	State level sport, officer and participated at state level in the school clubs	State level sport, officer of all school clubs	Winner for several competitions, several clubs
Junior	Academics and Grade	Medium to high challenging course 4.0 Unweighted	Courses that can increase weighted GPA 4.0 Unweighted	High challenging courses 3.8 Unweighted
	Extracurriculars	Continued the same sport and recognition at State/National level in the school club.	Added two seasonal sports, president of all clubs in school. Took up a service job in the local area.	Extracurriculars took precedence over academics. Added more wins to the profile and several clubs.

Senior	Academics and Grade	High Challenging Courses 4.0 Unweighted	Courses to boost GPA 4.0 Unweighted	High challenging courses 3.6 Unweighted
	Extracurriculars	Coach for the sport with disabl-ed kids. Helped another school in the area start their own FBLA and coached students. Recognition at the National level at DECA/FBLA and invited for national conferences.	Captain of sports, president of all clubs in school, and starting new clubs in the school.	Travelled world-wide for compe-titions. Founder of a non-profit organization.

How to Conduct Yourself Throughout High School

Passion and Depth

Pursue your interests with genuine passion and depth. Colleges value students who demonstrate dedication to their chosen activities.

Time Management

Balance academics, extracurriculars, and personal life by developing strong time management skills.

Seek Help

If you encounter academic challenges or need guidance, don't hesitate to seek help from teachers, counselors, or mentors.

Networking

Build meaningful relationships with teachers, counselors, and other students. Engage with professionals in fields that interest you.

Character and Integrity

Demonstrate good character, integrity, and ethical behavior in all aspects of your life. Be humble. Awards, recognitions, and grades will fade away, but our character and attitude will be remembered! Speak up and stand for what you believe in!

Resilience

College admissions can be competitive and stressful. Develop resilience to overcome setbacks, and keep pushing forward.

Remember, the college admissions process is holistic, and there's no one-size-fits-all approach. While these guidelines can significantly enhance your chances to be accepted into your dream school, when you look back, you will be proud that you stayed true to yourself and showcased your unique qualities and experiences throughout the application process, no matter the result.

When building your high school roadmap, remember these simple tips to stay focused and avoid distractions. First, set clear goals and plan to reach them step by step. Stick to your plan regardless of how difficult it gets. Surround yourself with supportive friends who cheer you on, like they're your biggest fans. Stay away from things that sidetrack you, like your phone or video games, during study time. Remember, it's okay to stumble sometimes, but get back up and keep going. Stay true to yourself, and believe in your potential. With dedication and a clear path, you'll rock your high school journey like a boss!

Parent Note: These years can make or break your student with the company they have, the support they get in and out of home, or their habits. It is very important to focus on your child's actions, and kindness counts every minute of the day for your student, no matter the circumstance. Some non-negotiable basic rules such as having good manners, giving time back, saying no to dangerous things, and working hard will stay with them longer than we think. As a family, sit together to understand their goals and support them wherever you can—whether it is driving them to an activity, finding a low-cost tutor, locating resources for academics, or doing background checks on adults whom they seek out for mentoring. Lastly, it is okay to help them with repeated mundane school tasks which are busy work—such as coloring and adding borders to a lab book—or with monitoring their grades monthly. Financial impacts and discussions are equally important so they understand their goals, activities, colleges, or scholarships they want to aim for. Keep track of their relationships outside homes and encourage them to find the right fit, stick to their passion, but be open to discussing others' likes, have a diverse social life, and take responsibility for their actions while keeping the big picture in mind. Take responsibility in protecting your child's intellectual properties and monitor for unethical competition from others in and out of the school. There are ups and downs as they navigate their high school. They change as a person trying to keep us happy. Our job is to understand their independence and letting go of their childhood dependence on us. It's important to give them the feeling that no matter what, we are ready to help them any time of the day, letting go of any of our priorities. Monitor their mood and offer your guidance to plan their time effectively. Social media and phones are a distraction, just like it for us adults. Have some ground rules for the family on using phones while at home and ensure the rule applies to all including ourselves. It is important to support and advocate for them if the student is trying their best, but at the same time, it's important to correct their actions if they take a wrong path.

SKILLS

*"I am always doing what I cannot do
yet, in order to learn how to do it."*

—VINCENT VAN GOGH

Description: *Your skills define who you are and are one of the biggest foundations for success in high school and even beyond. We will discuss skills such as obtaining time management, maintaining relationships, building a positive mindset, and understanding the importance of communication. Each of these individual aspects help build a strong person when applying for colleges and further round out your portfolio.*

CHAPTER 3

Time Management

Timing: Start in Middle School Years and
Continue Throughout High School

You're sitting in your third-period class, looking at your watch for the fifth time. It's only been twenty minutes, but it feels like six whole school days have passed. Suddenly you remember that you have a final project due by the end of the period, meaning you only have seventy minutes to complete a forty-five-page reading guide about World War II. Not an ideal situation.

But in your head, all the work is backed up. You didn't procrastinate, you just didn't have the time. Between soccer practice, student government, hanging out with your friends, piano lessons, and planning for your party this weekend, you just weren't able to get to your reading guide over the past few weeks. Sure, it makes sense to you, but it doesn't to your teacher, principal, parents, or peers.

This chapter discusses the importance of creating the time you need to balance everything, setting your goals and priorities, and identifying effective time allocation and management strategies to be the most successful version of yourself. We'll also discuss how to avoid procrastination and distractions and how to balance time for your personal growth and well-being.

Understanding Time Management

First of all, what is time management? Good time management is effectively organizing and prioritizing your time to accomplish tasks, responsibilities, and goals in a balanced and efficient manner. But it never stops there—good time management creates an incredible ripple effect for any teenager. When we look at the relationship between time management and personal success, we find it to be closely correlated. Effective time management enables teenagers to optimize their productivity, reduce stress, achieve academic success, pursue personal interests, get enough sleep, and maintain a healthy work-life balance. All of this contributes to making us overall significantly more successful and productive individuals.

Time Management for Admissions

I believe college admissions measure us subtly here on "Time Management" when they see our overall application. They want to know what we did with our time and resources. The book, *Grandfather's Gold Watch*, always resonates with me regarding time management. In the story, the protagonist is given a watch by his grandfather and is told to ask himself two questions every time he sees the watch—"What have you done with your name?" and "What have you done with your time?" These questions always remind the boy to be conscious of how he is using his time and remember where he needs to go. Anybody judging us or our capabilities is in a way looking for the answers to the same questions—what have we done with our time and name? They are gauging whether we have used it to learn, grow as an individual, and make a difference, and they are seeing whether we can continue doing this in our undergraduate and beyond. No one is looking for that one day when we took a break or one semester when we couldn't handle our grades. They are looking for a measurement of our learning quality, improving ourselves over the four years, and whether we have transformed into responsible adults.

It's important to realize the psychological and emotional toll that poor time management takes on us as young individuals:

1. **Stress and Anxiety:** Many teenagers face the challenge of the constant fear of deadlines, unfinished work, and lack of time to meet commitments which creates an overwhelming sense of anxiety when trying to complete work.

2. **Poor Self-Esteem:** Not being able to meet deadlines or achieve goals can create a negative image of yourself as someone who cannot get anything done, making it difficult to complete tasks.

3. **Reduced Quality:** Being on a rushed schedule due to procrastination and poor time management can lead to a big reduction in quality of work which consequently leads to decline in productivity because of the inability to stay motivated.

From a personal standpoint, I was never an expert at time management but I keep working on it. Time management is consistently a work in progress and something that each and every one of us can attempt to get better at every single day. Therefore, ensuring we're using the right tips and techniques to maximize our efficiency is important.

Assessing Current Time Management Habits

One of the time management process's first and most important steps is identifying strengths and weaknesses in the current approaches. I've tried to outline some steps to assess your current time management techniques.

Assessing current time management techniques is essential for teenagers to identify strengths and weaknesses in their approach.

Here are some steps to assess their current time management techniques:

Step 1: Self-Reflection

Let's start with self-reflection. Take the time to ask yourself some of these questions:

- How do you currently organize your time?
- What strategies or techniques do you use to manage your tasks and responsibilities?
- Are there specific areas where you need help managing your time effectively?
- How do you prioritize your activities and allocate time to different tasks?

These questions allow you to think about how you truly want to change your time management strategies or even decide you don't want to.

Step 2: Start a Time Log

If you can, keep a time log for a few days or weeks and take the time to record how you spend your time. Start with activities, tasks, and the duration of each. This log can help provide insights into how you currently manage your time.

Step 3: Identify Patterns

Review this time log and start to look for any patterns or trends that may be occurring. It would be best to start looking at ways you're wasting time, instances of procrastination, or any areas where you struggle to meet deadlines because of distractions.

Step 4: Task Completion

Now take a look at how you're able to complete tasks within an allotted time. This will allow you to identify if you often underestimate the time required for certain activities or frequently run out of time to finish important tasks. You can take help from your teachers or parents to measure an activity before and after.

Step 5: Productivity, Quality, and Feedback

See if you can receive feedback from teachers, parents, or mentors on your previous time management skills. On top of this, reflect on the quality of your work and ask yourself a few of these questions:

- Do you feel rushed or unsatisfied with the output? What do you do when you are not happy with your work?

- Did you need help to concentrate or stay focused? Do you always go to someone for help?

- Did you feel stressed or overwhelmed when you were trying to manage your time? What did you do when you felt this way?

Did you focus your time on mundane things that could have been efficient, on the bigger picture rather than on smaller details that were more personalized towards you?

Focusing on these specific assessment techniques makes it easier to understand your current strategies, which is a great starting step into creating effective time management strategies that meet your individual needs and goals.

Setting Goals and Priorities

I have always maintained a calendar plan every year with my academics and other community service goals to keep me on track. When I started high school, I usually spent the last few weeks in December during the winter break with my mom's guidance to create a plan, since most summer program applications open around the same time. This has helped me to keep track of how many tests do I have, what should I do for my summer and when should I give myself a break. Personally, I love visually appealing and clear plans so when I complete a goal, I get the satisfaction of marking it complete. I would review the same plan in summer to see if I need to adjust it again to fit my schedule. There are many tools where you can create this, but I personally like to see mine in Excel sheets.

Embrace Your Dreams and Passion

Take a moment to reflect on your dreams and passions. What makes you jump out of bed in the morning? Is it writing, painting, gaming, sports, or creating cool tech stuff? Identify what makes your heart skip a beat, and use that as the foundation for setting your goals.

Get SMART About It

Now that you've discovered your passions, it's time to turn those dreams into tangible goals.

Remember the SMART acronym:

- **Specific:** Be precise about what you want to achieve. Don't just say, "I wanna be a great artist." Instead, say, "I want to improve my sketching skills by practicing for at least an hour daily."

- **Measurable:** Track your progress! Break down your goal into smaller milestones and set measurable targets. This way, you'll be able to see how far you've come.

- **Achievable:** Set goals that are challenging yet doable. Don't aim to master guitar in a week if you've never touched one. Give yourself the time and space to grow.

- **Relevant:** Ensure that your goals align with your passions and aspirations. If you dream of becoming a filmmaker, there might be better uses of your time than spending hours perfecting your skateboarding skills (unless you plan to make a skateboarding documentary, of course!).

- **Time-bound:** Set deadlines to keep yourself motivated. Procrastination can sneak in and steal your dreams without a sense of urgency. Give yourself reasonable timeframes to achieve your goals and stick to them.

Prioritize Like a Pro

Start by identifying your high-priority tasks—the ones that'll impact your goals most. These are the things that absolutely cannot wait. Create a to-do list and then look at what is important and what's not. You can use cool apps or old-school planners. Or it can be a simple Excel sheet with categories—Primary, Secondary, and Tertiary.

Pro tip: Don't get caught up in the whirlwind of urgent but unimportant stuff. Be ruthless with your time and protect it like a prized possession. A TED Talk titled "An ER doctor on triaging your crazy busy life" by Daria Long, gave me a great tip of using the technique of an ER doctor to prioritize my life. They attend to the most critical patient first. They categorize their patients as Red— immediately life-threatening, Yellow—serious, but not immediately life-threatening and Green—minor.

This technique has helped me prioritize or triage the most critical things in a week.

Slice It Up

Have you ever heard of the Pomodoro Technique? It's a game-changer when it comes to managing your time effectively. Here's how it works: Set a timer for twenty-five minutes and work on a single task, giving it your full focus. Once the timer goes off, take a five-minute break to stretch, scroll Instagram, or grab a snack. Repeat this cycle three more times. After completing four cycles, reward yourself with a more extended break of fifteen to thirty minutes. Breaking your tasks into manageable chunks helps you stay focused, avoid burnout, and maintain productivity like a pro.

Learn the Art of Saying "No"

Repeat after me: "No, sorry, can't make it." Learning to say no is a crucial skill for effective time management. You can't do it all, and that's okay. Be selective about how you spend your time, and say yes to the things that align with your goals and priorities. Don't let FOMO get the best of you. Remember, every time you say no to something, you say yes to your dreams!

Reflect and Adjust

Finally, don't forget to take stock of your progress. Regularly review your goals, assess your achievements, and make adjustments if needed in a certain frequency. Life happens, and it's okay to tweak your goals. Be flexible, adapt, and keep pushing forward. Remember, it's your journey, and you're the captain of your time-management ship.

Creating a Time Management System

One of the most effective ways to manage time is to create a system. Something that can be consistent, repeatable, and planned around your own life. A time management system forces you to think ahead of time all the things we think usually at the last minute, and then makes it a process that you force yourself to stick to.

Following are some of the considerations as you build you own time management system.

Know Yourself

Before we dive into crafting a time management routine, it's essential to understand your unique rhythms and preferences. Are you a morning person full of energy at the crack of dawn? Or do you thrive during the late-night hours? Identify your peak productivity times, which will guide you in structuring your routine. I am not a morning person, but if I am speaking or conducting an innovation workshop for students in the other part of the globe, I will typically wake up early to accommodate their schedules. In this case I wouldn't mind waking up early because I am excited and motivated for the task.

Set Your Non-Negotiables

Start by identifying your non-negotiables—the activities that must be part of your routine no matter what. These can include school, extracurricular activities, family time, and hobbies. Determine the fixed blocks of time that are already accounted for in your day and mark them in your schedule.

Prioritize Tasks and Set Goal

Now that you clearly understand your non-negotiables, it's time to prioritize your tasks and set goals. Start by identifying the most important tasks that align with your short-term and long-term goals. Break them into actionable steps, and assign specific time slots in your routine. Remember, not all tasks are created equal. Focus on the ones that most directly impact your goals. Keep your priorities in mind, and allocate sufficient time to work on them.

Build in Breaks and Flexibility

You're not a robot, my friend! It's crucial to build in breaks and allow for flexibility in your routine. Breaks help you recharge, stay focused, and avoid burnout. Schedule short breaks between tasks to stretch, grab a snack, or do something you enjoy. Additionally, be open to adjusting your routine when unexpected events or opportunities arise. Flexibility is key to maintaining a healthy and balanced lifestyle. I have to play the piano every evening to take a break, so no matter what, I stop my homework and start playing to relax. I don't compete in piano competitions anymore, nor am I a professional pianist, but just the fact that I can be on my own and relax is an important skill that I learned over the years.

Create a Visual Schedule

Now it's time to bring your routine to life by creating a visual schedule. You can use a planner, a calendar app, or a whiteboard. Make it colorful and exciting, incorporating your style. Assign specific time slots to each activity or task, including your "nonnegotiable" assignments discussed earlier, study time, hobbies, and relaxation. Having a visual representation of your routine will help you stay organized and accountable.

Test and Iterate

Once you've created your initial time management routine, it's time to implement it. Keep track of how well it works for you. Pay attention to what flows smoothly and what needs adjustments. Be open to experimenting and iterating as you discover what works best for your unique needs and preferences.

Stay Disciplined and Adapt

Building a time management routine requires discipline and commitment. Stick to your schedule as much as possible, but forgive when life throws curveballs. Adaptability is key, so if something doesn't go according to plan, don't stress. Adjust, reschedule, and keep moving forward.

Reflect and Celebrate

Regularly reflect on your time management routine. Take note of what's working well, what needs improvement, and how it aligns with your goals. Celebrate your accomplishments, no matter how small they may seem. Recognize the progress you're making and the effort you're putting in. Remember, it's all about continuous improvement and finding the best routine for you.

You now have the tools to create your personal time management routine. Take charge of your time, make every moment count, and watch as you unlock new levels.

CHAPTER 4

Staying True to Yourself

Timing: Throughout High School
Years and Beyond

High school can be filled with ups and downs, and it's easy to get caught up in the expectations of others and lose sight of who we truly are. Staying true to ourselves is crucial for a fulfilling and authentic high school experience. This chapter explores practical ways to stay grounded and genuine while planning your high school journey, handling the success of others, and tackling the college application process.

Planning Your High School Journey

Embrace Your Passions and Interests

When plotting your high school roadmap, start by identifying your passions and interests. If you followed Chapter 1, you have already asked yourself what activities make your heart sing and bring you joy. Building your journey around what you love will keep you motivated and engaged throughout high school.

Set Personal Goals

To stay true to yourself, set clear and realistic personal goals. Don't just follow the crowd or aim for goals that don't resonate with your desires. Whether it's getting involved in community service, joining a club, or improving your grades, choose goals that align with your interests and values. This will help you stay focused and committed to your path.

Avoid Comparisons

It's easy to compare ourselves to others, especially when it comes to achievements and successes. Remember, everyone's journey is unique, and comparing yourself to others is like comparing apples and oranges. Stay in your lane and focus on your own progress. Celebrate your achievements, no matter how small they may seem, as they are a testament to your growth and efforts. The only person to compare is the "previous" you. You can definitely learn from others and get inspired, even celebrate others' achievements, but comparing and thinking negatively or trying to achieve the same or trying hard to copy others can lower our self-esteem and increase self-doubt in the long run.

Dealing with Others' Success

Celebrate Their Success

When you see others achieving great things, celebrate their accomplishments genuinely. Be happy for them and offer congratulations. A positive and supportive attitude towards others' success fosters a positive environment and builds meaningful connections with your peers.

Refrain from Jealousy

Feeling a tinge of jealousy is normal, but it's essential to recognize it and move past it. Instead of letting jealousy consume you, use it as motivation to work harder and achieve your own goals. Everyone has their strengths, and your unique talents will shine in due time. Be unique and better, not similar and sour running behind goals because someone achieved it.

Stay Focused on Your Journey

While it's great to appreciate others' achievements, avoid obsessing over them. Focus on your journey and how you can improve yourself. Each person's success story is different and comes at different times, and comparing yourself to others can be counterproductive. Stay committed to your path and trust in your abilities. If anything, learn from others' achievements. What worked well for them? What did they do differently from you? Should you try to do all those things or do you want to believe in your path? Success, whether it is yours or others can be an important learning moment. Extracurriculars and courses that worked for some other person, may not work for you because that's not where your passion lies. In the short-term you may find it as an easy and tested path, but in the long run, you may ruin your happiness running after something that gives you some instant reward or award.

CHAPTER 5

Forming Relationships

Timing: Throughout High School Years

Meeting and collaborating with the right peers, mentors, and teachers can make a profound difference in personal and academic growth. The power of relationships within educational environments cannot be overstated because they foster an environment of support, inspiration, and mutual learning. Let's talk about how these connections help shape us as people.

Building Strong Connections with Peers

Peers are the companions we share our educational voyage with who shape our perspectives and experiences. Students can find inspiration, encouragement, and constructive criticism by forging meaningful relationships with the right peers. Working collaboratively with like-minded individuals fosters a healthy competitive spirit that drives each group member to reach their fullest potential.

One significant advantage of connecting with peers is exchanging knowledge and skills. Each individual brings unique strengths and talents to the table, creating an environment conducive to continuous learning. As students share ideas, thoughts, and experiences, they gain new insights and broaden their horizons. This mutual learning cultivates camaraderie, making the academic journey more enriching and enjoyable.

Moreover, supportive peer connections are a strong support system during challenging times. The encouragement and empathy shared among peers build resilience and instill the belief that collective efforts can overcome obstacles. Working with the right people is equally important.

The Role of Mentors in Guiding the Way

Mentors are invaluable guides who offer wisdom, experience, and advice to navigate the complexities of academic and personal growth. Whether in formal mentorship programs or informal relationships, mentors provide a source of inspiration, motivation, and direction.

Mentors possess a wealth of knowledge accumulated through their own experiences. They act as a beacon of guidance, providing insights into various academic and career paths. By tapping into their expertise, students can make informed decisions about their future and identify opportunities for growth and development.

A vital aspect of mentorship is the individualized attention and support that mentors provide. They understand their mentees' unique strengths and weaknesses and tailor their guidance accordingly. This approach allows students to further build on their strengths and work on areas that need improvement, leading to a more focused learning experience.

Furthermore, mentors serve as role models, demonstrating perseverance, leadership, and integrity. Observing and emulating these traits positively influence students' personal growth and leadership skills. The mentor-mentee relationship fosters a sense of accountability, inspiring students to strive for excellence and take ownership of their actions.

Working Closely with Teachers

Teachers hold the power to shape the lives of their students profoundly. Beyond imparting knowledge, they cultivate critical thinking, creativity, and a love for learning. When students connect with inspiring teachers, their academic journey transforms into a voyage of discovery and enlightenment.

Exceptional teachers go beyond the curriculum, nurturing students' curiosity and passions. They create engaging and stimulating learning environments encouraging students to explore and question. By fostering a love for learning, inspiring teachers instill a lifelong hunger for knowledge and personal growth.

Moreover, supportive teachers advocate for their students, recognizing their strengths and providing constructive feedback for improvement. They nurture a growth mindset, empowering students to embrace challenges and view failures as stepping stones to success. The bond formed with such teachers creates a safe space where students can express their thoughts and ideas without fear of judgment.

How Does Collaboration Help Us?

A lot of times, we get stuck in our minds. Not exactly sure where to go with our ideas and plans, we undervalue the importance of forming connections with the right peers, mentors, and teachers, which can lead to extraordinary achievements together. Focusing on how collective intelligence and diverse perspectives can encourage us to step outside our comfort zones is important.

Think of collaboration as an opportunity for you to meet other people but also help realize your expertise. Each individual's strengths are amplified, creating an incredibly dynamic and supportive ecosystem. It's important to exchange ideas, value different viewpoints, and adapt to diverse perspectives. In addition, it creates sensitivity, empathy, open-mindedness, and flexibility—all important qualities to have in a constantly growing world.

However, collaboration doesn't just stop at classrooms with peers around you; in this chapter, we'll take the time to discuss how to cultivate and foster relationships with yourself, your peers, your teachers, your mentors, and your parents—all incredibly important parts of the journey of creating yourself and building your portfolio upwards.

Mentors and Teachers

These people should play a pivotal role in promoting collaboration. They can help facilitate an environment where students can learn from each other, but it also builds a sense of mutual respect that should last well beyond the classroom.

Peers

When you have a drive and motivation, constant support, motivation, and encouragement are needed, which comes from your friends and the crowd you surround yourself with.

Parents

Forming and keeping a good relationship with your parents intact allows you to go to someone for support. While you may want to take the college admissions process and all of the high school down your path, having the support of your parents doesn't hurt, especially in times of need. Time and again, if something didn't work for me, my parents were the first ones to guide me in the path to get me to where I want to.

Yourself

In this high-stress part of the process, it's equally important to respect and cultivate a good relationship with yourself, prepare yourself to collaborate, and stay open-minded to new possibilities.

Friends

High school can be an exciting yet challenging time in your life. It's when you explore your interests, build lasting friendships, and pave the way for your future. A crucial aspect of successfully navigating high school is developing strong relationships with peers. These connections can provide support, enhance your learning experience, and create a positive social environment. I want to explore strategies and tips on how to build meaningful relationships with your peers to thrive in high school.

Approachable and Friendly

Approachability is key when it comes to building relationships. Smile, maintain open body language, and show genuine interest in others. Be friendly and make an effort to initiate conversations with your classmates. Small acts of kindness—like greeting them, complimenting their achievements, or offering help—can create a positive impression.

Join Clubs and Extracurricular Activities

Being a part of clubs, sports, and other extracurricular activities is an excellent way to meet peers who share your interests. It provides opportunities to collaborate, learn, and bond over common goals. Choose activities that go hand in hand with your passion, and explore different groups to expand your social circle. Be an active participant and contribute positively to the group's dynamics.

Practice Active Listening

Developing good listening skills is essential for building strong relationships. When engaging in conversations with your peers, give them your undivided attention. Show empathy, be non-judgmental, and validate their thoughts and feelings. Ask follow-up questions and show genuine curiosity. By actively listening, you'll create an environment where people feel heard and understood, fostering deeper connections.

Collaborate and Offer Help

High school often involves group projects and assignments. Embrace these opportunities to collaborate with your peers. Be willing to contribute your ideas, respect others' opinions, and work together towards shared goals. Offer help when someone is struggling or needs assistance. Building a reputation as a reliable and supportive team member will earn your peers' respect and trust.

Say "No" Respectfully

You cannot be there everywhere for everyone or make everybody happy. Sometimes, saying no helps both your peers and yourself. Cut off from relations where you think it is unproductive or you are being taken advantage of. As a high school student, you have so much going on and handling unnecessary things is just a nuisance that you can deal with later in your life or when you may have free time in the summer.

Show Respect and Embrace Diversity

Any healthy and positive relationship leverages respect. Treat your peers with kindness, empathy, and respect. Embrace the diversity within your school community through appreciating different cultures, backgrounds, and perspectives. Avoid gossiping, bullying, or any negative behavior that can damage relationships. Encourage inclusivity and create a welcoming environment where everyone feels valued.

Foster Positivity and Encourage Others

Positivity is contagious, and you can influence the atmosphere around you by fostering a positive attitude. Offer words of encouragement, celebrate your peers' successes, and provide support during challenging times. Be a source of motivation and inspiration to others. Lifting others creates a positive cycle that benefits you and your peers.

Resolve Conflicts Constructively

Conflicts are inevitable in any relationship, but discussing how to handle them is important. When conflicts arise, address them calmly and respectfully. Seek understanding by actively listening to the other person's perspective. Find common ground and work towards a solution that benefits both parties. Avoid holding grudges or spreading negativity; it can damage relationships and hinder your high school experience. If you cannot resolve it and it does not impact your or the other person's goals, walk away amicably.

Building strong relationships with your peers is vital to high school success. These relationships provide a support system, enhance your learning experience, and contribute to a positive social environment. You can develop meaningful connections that will enrich your high school journey by being approachable, joining extracurricular activities, practicing active listening, collaborating, showing respect, fostering positivity, and resolving conflicts constructively. Remember, investing time and effort into building relationships will benefit your present and lay the foundation for future success.

Meaningful Relationship with Teachers

Developing strong relationships with your teachers enhances your high school experience and plays a significant role in your college preparation. Your teachers can provide guidance, mentorship, and valuable recommendations that can impact your college admissions process. This section will explore strategies and tips for building meaningful relationships with your teachers to thrive in high school and increase your chances of getting into a good college.

Show Genuine Interest and Enthusiasm

Demonstrate your genuine interest in the subjects taught by your teachers. Actively participate in class discussions, ask thoughtful questions, and show enthusiasm for learning. When teachers see your passion, they will be more likely to invest in your academic growth and offer additional support and guidance.

Attend Office Hours and Seek Help

Take advantage of your teachers' office hours or designated time for extra assistance. Visit them to seek clarification, discuss assignments, or delve deeper into the subject. By showing initiative and a commitment to your academic success, you demonstrate your dedication and create opportunities for personalized guidance.

Be Respectful and Professional

Treat your teachers with respect and professionalism at all times. Be punctual, attentive, and engaged during class. Avoid disruptive behavior and show appreciation for their expertise and efforts. Additionally, communicate respectfully in all interactions, whether in person, through email, or during class discussions.

Be Proactive and Self-Motivated

Take responsibility for your learning by being proactive and self-motivated. Complete assignments on time, come prepared to class, and strive for excellence in your work. Teachers who see your commitment and dedication are more likely to invest in your success and offer additional guidance or opportunities.

Seek Feedback and Act on It

Request feedback from your teachers on your assignments and performance. Welcome constructive criticism as an opportunity for growth and improvement. Act on the feedback by making necessary adjustments and demonstrating your commitment to continuous learning. Teachers appreciate students who take feedback seriously and try to grow academically.

Engage in Class Discussions

Active participation in class discussions demonstrates your interest and engagement in the subject matter. Contribute thoughtful insights, share relevant examples, and ask intelligent questions. Engaging in discussions enhances your understanding and signals to your teachers that you are actively involved and committed to the learning process.

Show Appreciation

Express your gratitude to your teachers for their dedication and guidance. A simple thank-you note, an email expressing your appreciation, or a genuine word of thanks after class can go a long way in building positive relationships. Recognize the effort and time they invest in their teaching and mentorship, and let them know how much you value their support.

Maintain Communication

Stay connected with your teachers outside of class. If you come across an interesting article or resource related to the subject, share it with them. Inform them about your academic achievements, extracurricular activities, and future aspirations. This open line of communication showcases your commitment to learning and keeps your teachers informed about your progress.

Take Advantage of Opportunities for Extra Learning

Seek additional learning opportunities outside the classroom related to your academic interests. Participate in academic competitions, attend workshops or seminars, and pursue independent research projects. Demonstrating your dedication to continuous learning shows your teachers that you are motivated and serious about your education.

Build Long-Term Relationships

Building relationships with your teachers should include more than just a single academic year. Aim to develop long-term connections by staying in touch with them even after you have completed their classes. Your teachers can provide valuable advice, mentorship, and recommendations for college applications and beyond.

Meaningful Relationship with Mentors

Building relationships with mentors and lab experts in high school can significantly enhance your academic growth, research opportunities, and college prospects. These individuals possess expertise, experience, and guidance that can contribute to your success. This chapter will explore strategies and tips for establishing meaningful relationships with mentors and lab experts, empowering you to excel in high school and increase your chances of getting into a good college.

Identify Potential Mentors and Lab Experts

Start by identifying potential mentors and lab experts who align with your academic interests and career goals. Look for teachers, professors, professionals, or researchers with expertise in your field. Seek guidance from your teachers, counselors, or online resources to identify individuals who can serve as valuable mentors or lab experts.

Introduce Yourself and Express Interest

Once you have identified potential mentors or lab experts, introduce yourself and express your interest in their work or expertise. Send a polite and concise email explaining who you are, your background, what you are interested in researching, and why you want to learn more from them. Communicate your intention to establish a mentorship or seek guidance in their lab.

Attend Research Seminars and Conferences

Participate in research seminars, conferences, and workshops related to your field. Events like these help to provide opportunities to network with experts in the field. Engage in meaningful conversations, ask questions, and show your enthusiasm for research. Attend poster sessions and presentations to learn about ongoing projects and seek potential mentors or lab experts.

Seek Guidance and Advice

Approach potential mentors or lab experts for guidance and advice. Share your academic and research goals, and ask for suggestions on achieving them. Be prepared with specific questions or topics you would like to discuss. By seeking their expertise, you demonstrate your commitment to learning and willingness to benefit from their guidance.

Embrace Mentorship Opportunities

If a mentor or lab expert offers to guide you or provide mentorship, embrace the opportunity wholeheartedly. Make the most of their knowledge, experience, and support. Actively seek their feedback on your research ideas, projects, or academic pursuits. Be receptive to constructive criticism and incorporate their suggestions into your work.

Be a Responsible and Dedicated Learner

Demonstrate responsibility and dedication in your work as a mentee or lab assistant. Show up on time, meet deadlines, and take ownership of your tasks. Be proactive and independent in your research or lab work, seeking guidance when needed. By displaying a strong work ethic, you earn your mentor's and lab expert's respect and trust.

Build a Professional Relationship

Approach the mentor–mentee or lab expert relationship with professionalism. Respect their time and boundaries, and maintain confidentiality when required. Communicate effectively and professionally through email, meetings, or lab interactions. Show appreciation for their guidance and expertise, and express gratitude for the opportunities provided.

Contribute to Their Work

Find ways to contribute to your mentor's or lab expert's projects or research. Offer assistance through data collection, analysis, literature reviews, or experimental work. You demonstrate your commitment, initiative, and value as a mentee or lab assistant by actively contributing to their work.

Seek Additional Learning Opportunities

Request suggestions from your mentors or lab experts on additional learning opportunities, such as workshops, internships, or research programs. Actively pursue these opportunities to expand your knowledge and skills. Share your experiences with your mentors, seeking their guidance and feedback on how to maximize your learning.

Maintain Long-Term Connections

Building relationships with mentors and lab experts should extend beyond high school. Stay in touch even after you have completed your projects or research work. Chances are you can help them in ways you didn't think you could and you may get a way to express thanks in return for their guidance.

How to Request Flexibility

Balancing academics, extracurricular activities, and athletics can be challenging for high school students. However, with effective communication and a well-thought-out approach, asking for flexibility in school to pursue your passions outside the classroom is possible. This section will explore strategies to approach this conversation with school administrators, teachers, and coaches to create a harmonious schedule that allows you to excel academically and in your extracurricular pursuits.

Understand Your Priorities

Before initiating a conversation about flexibility:

1. Take the time to understand your priorities.
2. Assess the importance of your extracurricular activities and athletics in relation to your academic goals.
3. Consider how they contribute to your personal growth, character development, and future aspirations. This un-

derstanding will help you articulate your needs more effectively.

Research School Policies

Familiarize yourself with the school's policies regarding extracurricular activities and athletics. Understand any existing guidelines or requirements for participation and how they may impact your schedule. By being well-informed, you can present your request in a way that aligns with the school's policies and guidelines.

Schedule a Meeting

Request a meeting with the appropriate individuals, such as your guidance counselor, teacher(s), or school administrator(s), to discuss your request for flexibility. Choose a time when they will likely be available and not overwhelmed with other responsibilities. Ensure that you approach the meeting with a respectful and professional demeanor.

Articulate the Benefits

Clearly express the benefits of your extracurricular activities and athletics. Highlight how they contribute to your personal growth, leadership skills, teamwork abilities, and well-being. Emphasize their positive impact on your character development and their potential to enhance your college applications or future career opportunities.

Provide a Comprehensive Schedule

Create a comprehensive schedule demonstrating how you plan to manage your academic workload while participating in extracurricular activities and athletics. Show that you have thoughtfully considered the time commitment required for each activity and have strategized ways to balance your responsibilities effectively. This schedule should reflect your commitment to academic excellence and extracurricular pursuits.

Show Academic Preparedness

Assure school administrators, teachers, and coaches that you are prepared to handle the academic workload despite your extracurricular activities and athletics involvement. Share examples of your time management skills, organizational strategies, and past academic achievements demonstrating your ability to succeed.

Demonstrate Responsibility

Illustrate your responsible approach to managing your commitments. Share instances where you have successfully balanced your academic responsibilities with extracurricular activities or athletics in the past. Make sure to draw attention to how you're able to prioritize tasks, meet deadlines, and maintain open communication with teachers and coaches.

Propose Solutions

Offer potential solutions that address any concerns about missed classes or conflicting schedules. Propose alternative study arrangements, such as independent study or designated tutoring sessions, to ensure you stay on track academically. Suggest effective communication and coordination methods between teachers and coaches to minimize disruptions and ensure a smooth transition between commitments.

Discuss Support Systems

Share details about the support systems available to you. Talk about the involvement of your parents or guardians, who can provide transportation or help with time management strategies. Highlight the support of your coaches or advisors who can attest to your commitment and work with you to find suitable solutions.

Maintain Open Communication

After discussing your request, communicate openly with school administrators, teachers, and coaches. Update them regularly on your progress, discuss any challenges, and seek guidance when needed. This ongoing communication will foster understanding and trust among all parties involved.

Finding Mentors

Identify Your Interests

Before embarking on the search for a mentor, it's crucial to identify your areas of interest. Reflect on your passions, academic subjects, and career aspirations. This self-assessment will help you target mentors who align with your goals.

Utilize School Resources

Start your search for mentors within your high school. Teachers, guidance counselors, and faculty members can often mentor or connect you with professionals in your desired field. Explore extra-curricular clubs, honor societies, or academic departments focusing on your interests.

Online Platforms

Online platforms like LinkedIn, research databases, and social media can be excellent resources for finding mentors. Join professional groups, follow experts in your field, and reach out to individuals who inspire you. Look for mentorship programs specifically designed for high school students, such as those offered by universities or organizations.

Networking Events

Attend conferences, seminars, or workshops related to your interests. You will be able to meet researchers who can potentially become mentors. Engage in conversations, ask insightful questions, and express your enthusiasm for their work.

Crafting Effective Mentorship Emails

Introduction

When reaching out to potential mentors, making a strong first impression is essential. Your email should be concise and respectful, demonstrating your genuine interest in their work. Begin with a personalized salutation, addressing them by their name.

Express Interest

Clearly articulate why you are interested in their field of work or research. Highlight specific projects or publications of theirs that caught your attention. Show that you have done your homework and are genuinely passionate about your expertise.

State Your Intentions

Clearly state your purpose for reaching out, whether seeking mentorship, advice, or an opportunity to collaborate on a project. Be specific about what you hope to gain from the mentorship and how it aligns with your goals.

Highlight Your Qualifications

Briefly mention your relevant academic achievements, extracurricular activities, or previous experience showcasing your commitment and skills. Demonstrate how you want to learn and grow in your chosen field.

Request a Meeting

Politely request a meeting or a call to discuss mentorship opportunities further. Provide your availability and suggest a few options for convenience. Be flexible and understanding of their busy schedules.

Politeness and Gratitude

Conclude your email with a polite closing, expressing gratitude for their time and consideration. Use a professional sign-off, such as "sincerely" or "best regards," followed by your name and contact information.

Working with Mentors

Setting Expectations

Once you find a mentor, it's important to have a transparent conversation with them about what you expect and will provide them. Discuss the frequency and duration of meetings, preferred modes of communication, and the specific areas you hope to focus on.

Actively Seek Guidance

Take the initiative in seeking guidance from your mentor. Come prepared with questions, topics for discussion, or specific challenges you'd like assistance with.

Study Groups and Peers

The educational journey is not solitary. Rather, it thrives on collaboration, interaction, and mutual support. Among the many aspects that enrich the learning experience, study groups and peer interactions hold a unique and influential position. These powerful tools allow students to engage in collaborative learning, exchange ideas, and collectively enhance their understanding of various subjects. This part explores the significance of study groups and the impact of peer interactions on academic achievement, cognitive development, and social-emotional well-being. By shedding light on the advantages and benefits of these collaborative learning approaches, we uncover their profound influence on students' personal growth and success in their educational pursuits.

Understanding Study Groups

Study groups, often known as collaborative learning or peer study sessions, are small gatherings of students who come together to study, discuss, and learn collectively. These groups can be formal or informal, with their primary purpose being to supplement individual learning and create a space for interactive and engaging study experiences.

The Essence of Collaborative Learning

Collaborative learning in study groups is founded on the principle that knowledge is not a fixed entity but a dynamic process that evolves through social interaction. Engaging in discussions, exchanging ideas, and solving problems as a group encourages critical thinking, enhances understanding, and stimulates creativity.

The Role of Study Groups in Academic Environments

Study groups play a vital role in academic environments by fostering a culture of cooperation, peer support, and shared learning. Educators may encourage students to form study groups in formal settings to promote active learning and enhance their understanding of course materials. Furthermore, study groups allow students to work on challenging assignments together, reinforcing their comprehension and problem-solving skills.

The Impact of Peer Interactions on Academic Achievement

One of the most significant benefits of peer interactions lies in the motivation and accountability it instills in students. Within study groups, learners set collective goals, supporting and encouraging one another to perform at their best. The sense of accountability to their peers acts as a driving force, ensuring that students remain focused and committed to their academic pursuits.

Peer Tutoring and Explaining Concepts

In the context of study groups, students often take on the role of peer tutors, assisting their fellow learners in understanding complex concepts. Explaining ideas to others reinforces one's understanding, and students benefit from varied teaching styles within the group. This collaborative approach deepens comprehension and fosters leadership and communication skills among the peers who take on tutoring roles.

Building Confidence

Participating in study groups fosters a sense of confidence in students. The supportive and inclusive environment allows individuals to voice their ideas, seek clarification, and express their thoughts without fear of judgment. As students actively engage with their peers, they gain confidence in their academic and social abilities.

Peer Learning and Cognitive Development

The essence of peer interactions in study groups aligns with the principles of social constructivism, a learning theory pioneered by Lev Vygotsky. According to this theory, learning is a social process through interactions. In the context of study groups, students construct knowledge collectively through shared experiences, discussions, and reflections.

Zone of Proximal Development (ZPD)

Within study groups, students operate within their Zone of Proximal Development (ZPD), introduced by Vygotsky. The ZPD refers to the range of tasks that individuals can perform with the help of more knowledgeable peers or mentors. As students collaborate in study groups, they build on one another's learning, which looks at what can be done individually and what can be achieved with guidance.

Cognitive Apprenticeship

Participating in study groups resembles a form of cognitive apprenticeship. As students interact with their peers, they often learn from those with greater expertise or experience in certain subjects. This cognitive apprenticeship nurtures the growth and mastery of complex skills, providing learners with valuable insights and alternative perspectives on various topics.

Social and Emotional Benefits of Peer Interactions

Peers and friends are part of our ecosystem. Peer interactions contribute to our social and emotional development by enhancing communication skills, empathy, and a sense of belonging. Engaging with peers provides opportunities for emotional support, collaboration, and the cultivation of interpersonal relationships, which are crucial for our overall well-being during our high school years. Even though I had a loaded travel schedule which took me to some global conferences, I would long to come back home to meet my friends and share my experiences and find out all the fun events I missed in school while I was away.

Building Social Connections

Beyond academics, peer interactions in study groups foster student social connections. These connections create a sense of camaraderie and friendship, making the educational journey more enjoyable and fulfilling. Engaging in meaningful discussions and collaborative activities enables students to forge lasting connections beyond the classroom.

Reducing Academic-Related Stress

Peer interactions within study groups can significantly reduce academic stress. The presence of supportive peers offers students a platform to share their concerns, seek assistance, and discuss challenges openly. Through shared experiences and mutual support, students develop resilience and coping mechanisms contributing to overall well-being.

Enhancing Emotional Intelligence

Interacting with peers in study groups also fosters emotional intelligence. Students learn to understand and empathize with their peers' perspectives and emotions, nurturing a sense of emotional maturity and social awareness. These skills are important when looking at the ins and outs of relationships, both in academic and real-world settings.

Studying effectively and building strong academic foundations are crucial for gaining admission to a good college. One powerful tool at your disposal is creating study groups and leveraging the resources of your peers. In this portion, we will explore strategies for forming study groups, utilizing peer resources, and optimizing these collaborations to enhance your learning, generate innovative ideas, and excel in exams.

Forming Study Groups

Study groups can be effective if we have a clear goal and objectives. It can be a short-term objective of completing practice sets or a long-term objective of getting ready for the final exam. I personally loved taking a break from preparing for quizzes myself and form study groups that motivated me and provided the opportunity to reinforce understanding of a difficult concept.

Identify Compatible Peers

Seek classmates demonstrating dedication, motivation, and a shared commitment to academic success. Look for individuals who excel in subjects you struggle with, as their strengths can complement your weaknesses.

Establish Group Goals

Define the purpose and goals of your study group. Is it to share knowledge, discuss challenging concepts, or solve practice problems together? Establishing a common objective will ensure everyone is aligned and committed.

Set Meeting Schedule

Determine a regular meeting schedule accommodating everyone's availability. Consider creating a shared calendar or using online scheduling tools to simplify the process. Consistency is key to building a productive study group.

Establish Group Norms

Discuss and agree upon guidelines for participation, punctuality, respectful communication, and shared responsibilities. Establishing a supportive and inclusive environment will foster collaboration and enhance learning.

Utilizing Peer Resources

I am so grateful to my peer groups and their support with resources when I was away from school. My knowledge of a subject expanded exponentially if I took turns in explaining what I learned to others. Class notes and pictures of class-boards were common in our peer groups so each one of us can refer to it as and when we complete our assignments.

Share Class Notes and Resources

Pool together class notes, handouts, textbooks, and supplementary materials. Create a shared digital repository or use cloud-based platforms like Google Drive to facilitate easy access and collaboration.

Teach and Explain Concepts

Take turns explaining difficult concepts to each other. Teaching others solidifies your understanding and helps your peers grasp complex topics. Encourage open discussions and clarify any misconceptions collectively.

Discuss Assignments and Projects

Collaborate on assignments and projects by discussing ideas, brainstorming approaches, and providing feedback. Leverage the diverse perspectives within the group to generate innovative and well-rounded solutions.

Peer-to-Peer Tutoring

Offer to tutor each other in areas of strength. By teaching your peers, you reinforce your knowledge and understand the subject further. This practice also strengthens your communication and leadership skills.

Optimizing Study Group Effectiveness

Study groups can enhance learning through collaborative discussions, allowing members to share diverse perspectives and insights. The interactive nature of study groups promotes active engagement with the material, leading to better retention and understanding. Additionally, group members can provide support and motivation, fostering a conducive environment for academic success.

Active Participation

Engage actively during study group sessions. Contribute ideas, ask questions, and challenge each other's thinking. Actively listening to your peers and providing constructive feedback fosters a dynamic and enriching learning environment.

Establish Study Goals

Set specific study goals for each session. Focus on challenging topics, upcoming exams, or problem-solving exercises. Create a study plan with clear objectives to maximize productivity and track progress.

Divide and Conquer

Allocate tasks and responsibilities among group members. Divide study material, practice questions, or research topics to cover a broader range of content. Sharing the workload ensures efficient use of time and resources.

Practice Effective Communication

Communicate regularly outside of study group meetings. Utilize group messaging apps or email to share important updates, send out resources, and discuss study-related queries. Effective communication strengthens cohesion and collaboration.

Practice Exam Simulations

Conduct mock exams or practice tests within the study group. Mimicking exam conditions helps build familiarity, reduces anxiety, and provides opportunities for peer feedback. Evaluate performance collectively and identify areas for improvement.

CHAPTER 6

Maintaining a Positive Mindset/Mental Health

Timing: Throughout High School
Years and Beyond

Embracing your emotions while building a good high school portfolio and managing mental health and burnout is crucial for success. I personally have faced weeks where I had so much to do that, I lost motivation to start on anything. This in turn would make me grumpy the whole week. Then I also had days where I would plan everything for weeks in advance and be ahead.

Here are some tips to help you navigate this process:

Acknowledge and Accept Emotions

Recognize that emotions are a natural part of being human. Whether you experience excitement, anxiety, stress, or frustration during the four years, know it's okay to feel these emotions. Avoid suppressing them; acknowledge and accept them as valid responses to your challenges.

On the science side, once my doctor told me that our teenage brain goes through extensive remodeling, and the maturity of understanding total cause and effect happens only in the mid-twenties. That possibly explains David Elkind's theory of adolescent egocentrism, where *we* are the hero of our story; we just see our perspectives, and nothing wrong can ever happen to us, no matter our decisions. Typically, teenagers like you and me believe we are invincible and any risky behavior is fine, even if it means it hurts us or someone else.

To combat this easily in my mind, the general rule that my parents shared with me was, "If I feel I am doing something for pleasure, I am forsaking happiness in the long run. So it's important to understand the difference between pleasure and happiness." This could be applied to all aspects of our daily schedule: eating, social, texting, T.V., phone use, study, cleaning, driving habits; forming relationships; ethics; and many more. Eighty percent of the time, I would play this sentence in my mind and fix myself, and 20 percent, I would play this sentence and ignore it since the pleasure was too addicting to let go of. That is fine. It would be best to focus on your goals. Living daily as a teenager causes many emotions and conflicts in our brains, which we need to accept and move on.

Set Realistic Goals

We discussed this when defining SMART goals. The idea is to break down the tasks into manageable steps to avoid feeling over-whelmed. Be mindful of your mental and emotional capacity, and avoid overloading yourself with unrealistic expectations.

Find a Creative Outlet

Participate in a creative activity that helps you express your emotions. Whether painting, writing, or playing music, a creative outlet can be a healthy way to process feelings and reduce stress. There are days I loved playing the piano or bass guitar after completing my homework to give myself a brain break.

Practice Self-Compassion

Be kind to yourself. It's okay to make mistakes or face setbacks during high school years. Treat yourself with the same understand-ing and support you would offer a friend.

Reach Out for Support

Don't hesitate to seek support from friends, family, or teachers. Discuss your emotions and challenges openly with someone you trust. Sometimes sharing your feelings can provide relief and offer a fresh perspective.

Create a Balanced Schedule

Design a well-balanced schedule that includes time for portfo-lio work, academic studies, relaxation, and social activities. Avoid overcommitting and ensure you have enough time for self-care and rest. Effective time management with tips from the earlier chapter can help reduce stress and prevent burnout. Prioritize tasks, set deadlines, and create a study routine that allows for both activities and academic commitments.

Practice Mindfulness and Meditation

Engage in mindfulness practices or meditation to stay present and manage stress. Some version of staying true to your mental health is incredibly important.

Take Breaks When Needed

Listen to your body and mind. If you feel overwhelmed or exhausted, take a break. Stepping away from your activity or work briefly can recharge your energy and creativity.

Seek Professional Help

It's common for mental health to be super stigmatized, but there's no shame in asking for support, and they can provide valuable strategies to manage stress and emotions effectively. It could be your school guidance counselor or your doctor. Most schools today have a guidance counselor; speak to them if necessary. They may help resolve conflict with your teachers or peers.

Reflect on Your Progress and Growth

Take moments to reflect on your progress and the skills you've developed. Recognize your achievements, both big and small, and celebrate your growth.

Stay Organized

Keep track of your portfolio materials, graduation requirements, deadlines, and feedback you receive. Staying organized can help reduce anxiety and ensure you're on track with your goals.

Building a high school portfolio is just one aspect of your life, and your mental well-being is paramount. By embracing your emotions, seeking support when needed, and practicing self-care, you can navigate the high school years more effectively while safeguarding your mental health.

Discovering your dream school to maintain a positive mindset beyond high school is a highly personal and individual process. It requires introspection, research, and an understanding your unique aspirations and values. Your wellness is not confined to four years of high school, but continues beyond that. Here are some steps to help identify your dream school:

Reflect on Your Goals and Values

Consider your academic and career goals, personal values, and what you want to achieve in your college experience. Think about the type of environment, campus culture, peers, and academic programs that align with your aspirations.

Research Different Colleges and Universities

When exploring various colleges and universities, look into their academic offerings, extracurricular activities, campus life, and location. Compare their values and mission with your own to see if there is a good fit. Understand what you liked in your high school and what you did not. Add those as factors for the next four years and beyond.

In the next few sections, we will dig into each of the factors you will need to consider when making the decision to apply.

Research Location

Apart from the usual research of the location of the school for its urban, sub-urban or rural settings, there are several other factors to consider, Proximity to your most visited place, libraries, airports, and weather-climate allergies that affect you are all important when selecting a university and these factors vary in importance depending on the individual. Did you like going to school in winter? How was your mood? Do you want the same for the next four to six years? Did you like the urban/rural feeling? Do you want to change that? These are important factors that teachers, college counselors, and parents may be unable to help you with.

Visit Campus or Attend Virtual Tours

If you can, visit the campuses of schools you are interested in. Get a feel for the atmosphere, talk to current students, and attend information sessions. If in-person visits are not possible, participate in virtual tours and online events. Research online to get a feel of the place. Most universities market themselves but go outside the university website to find the feel of the place.

Consider Your Preferred Major or Field of Study

If you have a specific major or field of study in mind, research the programs offered by different schools. Look for institutions with strong departments in your area of interest. US college rankings are not the best way to determine the departments in your area of interest. Resources, ease of research or internship opportunities, collaborations with local organizations and industries, published papers, a Google search on the number of times the department has been in the news, and newsletters give you a feel of the program's quality.

Evaluate Extracurricular Opportunities

Think about the extracurricular activities that matter to you. Whether it's sports, arts, community service, or other clubs, ensure the schools you're considering offer opportunities to engage in activities you're passionate about. It should be easy for you to get in and should have backup options if you don't get in. Pre-professional extracurriculars and clubs, which again feel like a competitive college admission process, are many times not worth it. I know of schools where pre-professional clubs are so competitive that the application process is exhausting, have single-digit acceptance rates, and both grad/undergrad students compete. Is that worth your time? Maybe for some of them, but in my case, I will lose the passion to be part of the club if all I have to do is apply consistently and show my worth in something I enjoy. You cannot escape the competitive nature, but you can look for universities with a backup option. Suppose I do not get into the theatre club with auditions. In that case, I have another performing arts club or activity, which may be less competitive.

Assess Financial Fit

Consider the financial aspect of attending college. Evaluate scholarships, financial aid packages, and the overall cost of attendance. Find a school that aligns with your financial needs and goals. Discuss with your parents how much they can afford, how much you have to care for, and find the best fit. I have friends who spent all their application time and high school years aiming for a particular university just to get accepted and then finding out they could not afford it, did not apply for scholarships earlier, and had to depend completely on their parents. However, do not use the financial aspect as an excuse not to try for your dream school. There are scholarships that you can apply for. Seek your high school counselor or parents to search for scholarships and provide you with the deadlines so that you can apply earlier.

Talk to Alumni and Current Students

Reach out to alums and current students from schools you are interested in. They can typically give you a better understanding of what to expect. Current students usually like to say nice things about their decisions and their universities, so they may not be a reliable source if questions are not pointed and are general; however, asking explicit questions such as what did you not like and what could you have seen better will give you a feeling of the pros and cons so that you can make a decision.

Remember that your dream school should reflect your preferences and aspirations. Avoid getting swayed by external influences or the choices of your friends. What matters most is finding a school that feels right for you.

Here's why your dream school might differ from your friends:

Different Academic Goals

You and your friends may have different academic interests and career aspirations, leading you to prefer schools with distinct programs and opportunities.

Unique Personal Values

Your values and priorities may differ from your friends. Some students may prioritize a school's reputation or size, while you might value factors like campus culture and community.

Location Preferences

Your ideal college location might be different from your friends. Some students prefer urban environments, while others may be drawn to rural or suburban campuses. Weather is a huge factor for many who prefer seasons or warm temperatures.

Extracurricular and Social Preferences

The extracurricular activities and campus social scene that excite you may differ from your friends. Everyone has their interests and ways of engaging with college life.

Financial Considerations

Financial circumstances play a significant role in college choices. Your dream school might differ from your friends' due to varying financial needs and available resources. For example, you may or may not be able to afford a certain school. Or, you don't want to take loans to pay for college.

Family or Cultural Influences

Family expectations, cultural influences, or unique life experiences can also shape your preferences for a dream school, which may differ from those of your friends. Families with legacy or have tax benefits with certain universities, might have a vested interest in you applying to the school of their preference.

Remember that choosing a college is a personal decision; there is no one-size-fits-all answer. Trust yourself, follow your instincts, and find the school that resonates with your goals and values. Your dream school should be where you can thrive academically, personally, and socially, setting you up for a successful and fulfilling college experience.

Staying Positive During Application Season

Maintaining a positive and realistic mindset during college application is essential for teenagers. It's important to approach this phase optimistically while staying grounded in reality.

Here are some strategies to help you cultivate a positive yet realistic mindset:

Focus on the Process

Instead of fixating solely on the result—getting into a specific college—shift your focus to the process of self-discovery and personal growth. View college applications as an opportunity to learn more about yourself, your interests, and your goals. All admissions are looking for is if you have the training, stamina, passion, right attitude, best of character, and purpose to be part of their team. Embrace the journey and value the experiences and skills you gain.

Remember that the college application is about finding the right fit for your future, not just about getting into a prestigious institution.

I found some guides for the schools I wanted to be part of and did my best to know them and provide enough information for them to know me. It was like a two-sided interview without meeting each other in person.

There are several blogs, guides and vlogs for many other universities. Sometimes I found a one-stop shop guide from the university, so you don't have to read lists and lists of websites. Most guides give us the message that "Don't try too hard to admit yourself, but be yourself, show us your passion and we will decide the rest."

Celebrate Small Victories

Acknowledge and celebrate each achievement throughout the college application process. Completing an application, receiving a positive recommendation, achieving a high score on standardized tests, or even writing a compelling essay are all milestones worth recognizing. By celebrating small victories, you build momentum and maintain a positive outlook. Recognize that every step forward brings you closer to your goals.

Practice Self-Compassion

Be kind to yourself and remember that the college application process is challenging for most students and is a puzzle. It is especially important for students whose parents were educated outside of the US. It adds to the challenge of educating them and yourselves on what is important and what is not. Avoid comparing yourself to others and their essays, and focus on your strengths and accomplishments. Treat yourself with understanding and forgiveness, especially during stress or disappointment. Remember that setbacks and rejections are not reflections of your worth or potential. Instead of dwelling on failures, learn from them and use them as motivation to improve. As you are filling in your applications, there may be many mundane tasks such as checking transcripts, copying transcripts into your application, confirming you are graduating with all requirements, working on the next set of courses for second term, prioritizing activities that you want to share in the application, or focusing on completing non-essential application details such as address, information about parents, scores, and other optional information. Instead of using your brain power all the time, request your high school counselor, your parents, or siblings to review and double-check these. I bribed my younger brother with boba to recheck my course names, years, and grades for my University of California application since I had dual enrollment, concurrent enrollment, and independent and school courses in my transcript. He was nine but did a fantastic job finding the mistakes due to fat-fingering and loved the fact that he was pointing at my mistakes.

Set Realistic Expectations

While it's important to dream big, setting realistic expectations is equally crucial. Understand that college admissions can be competitive, and acceptance rates vary. Research and identify a range of colleges that align with your academic profile, interests, and goals. This balanced approach allows you to aim high while considering more realistic options. Keep in mind that college admissions decisions are influenced by numerous factors beyond your control, such as institutional needs and applicant pools. By diversifying your college choices, you increase your chances of finding the right fit. Do not obsess over a college name and its ranking.

Embrace Rejection as Redirection

Receiving rejection letters can be disheartening, but it's essential to see them as redirection rather than failure. Understand that college admissions decisions are complex and often subjective. Rejection doesn't makeup who you are or define your worth. Take this as an opportunity to think about the goals you have in place, explore alternative paths, or consider different colleges that may be a better fit for your dreams. Success is never linear, and attending a particular college does not determine your future achievements.

If someone has rejected you, there may be a reason or acknowledgment that someone else is better than you, which we will always face. It is easy to define yourself as a victim and blame it on your circumstance, race, identity, lack of legacy, and many more. It is also easy to start a negative mindset on why others got in, not you. It is a natural reaction, but we don't have control over any of these, and we are just a small drop in this ocean of university acceptances. The only control we have is choosing another path that fits us and being ready to accept that challenge.

Seek Support and Perspective

Surround yourself with a support system that includes family, friends, teachers, and mentors who can provide guidance and a fresh perspective. Engage in open and honest conversations about your hopes, fears, and aspirations. Their insights and encouragement can help you maintain a positive and realistic mindset. Remember that you are not alone in this process and that seeking support is a sign of strength, not weakness.

Practice Mindfulness and Self-Care

Incorporate mindfulness techniques and self-care activities into your daily routine. Engaging in activities such as meditation, journaling, exercise, or pursuing hobbies can help reduce stress and maintain a positive mindset. Paying just as much attention to your mental and physical health is extremely important. Remember to prioritize self-care, sleep, eat healthily, and try to participate in activities that make you happy and relaxed. It's important to balance working hard on your applications and caring for yourself.

Remember the Bigger Picture

College admissions is just one chapter of your life's journey. My parents always said that college /undergraduate life was just an average of 5 to 7 percent of our life span, and while this will define some career paths, it goes by very fast. Remember that your worth and potential extend beyond the college application process. Recognize that personal growth, resilience, and character development are as valuable as admission to a specific college. Trust in your abilities and know that there are multiple pathways to success. The college you attend does not determine your future success; your dedication, passion, and drive will shape your path. Remember that success can be achieved in various ways, and the college experience is what you make of it.

A friend of mine had a clear path and co-founded an online school for middle and high school students with an innovative curriculum. He has his goal of expanding the school globally, and his high school and college education just supported him in expanding his skill set in school administration and expansion. I respect that he knew his purpose and focused on that with a clear vision, and I hope we all can learn from him that college is just the beginning of enhancing the skill set for a career.

Summary

Adopting a positive mindset and balancing it with a realistic outlook allows you to navigate the college application process with confidence, resilience, and self-assurance. Embrace the opportunities for growth and learning, celebrate your achievements, and remember that your worth extends far beyond the admissions decisions of any particular college. Focus on finding the right fit for your goals and aspirations, and trust your ability to create a bright future.

CHAPTER 7

Communication with Others

Timing: Throughout High School
Years and Beyond

In high school, communication with others plays a pivotal role in a student's personal growth and academic journey. Effective communication skills foster interpersonal relationships, encourage collaboration, and provide opportunities to showcase one's abilities. This chapter aims to explore the significance of communication in high school and its impact on creating a robust portfolio for college applications.

Social Development and Emotional Well-Being

Effective communication with peers, teachers, and mentors helps high school students develop essential social skills. Engaging in conversations, actively listening, and expressing thoughts and feelings build empathy and understanding, contributing to the overall emotional well-being of an individual. Social competence not only enhances personal relationships but also prepares students for future interactions in diverse professional settings.

Academic Success and Learning Opportunities

By participating actively in class discussions and clarifying doubts, students can grasp concepts more effectively. Collaborative projects and group activities offer opportunities to share ideas, work together, and learn from diverse perspectives. Effective communication also aids in seeking help from teachers or peers, enabling students to excel in their studies.

Networking and Extracurricular Engagement

High school is an ideal time to engage in extracurricular activities that align with one's interests and passions. Communication skills are instrumental in networking with clubs, organizations, and community initiatives. Students who actively communicate with others in these activities not only broaden their horizons but also demonstrate their dedication and leadership qualities, making their college applications stand out.

Personal Branding and Leadership

Through effective communication, students can establish a positive personal brand. Engaging in public speaking, joining debates, or participating in school events allows them to showcase their confidence and leadership abilities. This promotes a sense of identity and authenticity, making a significant impact on college admissions officers seeking well-rounded candidates.

Building Strong Letters of Recommendation

Effective communication with teachers and mentors nurtures strong relationships, leading to impressive letters of recommendation for college applications. When educators can attest to a student's communication skills, work ethic, and character, it reinforces their credibility and significantly enhances the student's portfolio.

Teamwork and Collaboration

High school projects often involve teamwork and collaboration. Students who can communicate ideas clearly and respectfully contribute positively to group dynamics. This ability to work collaboratively and communicate effectively is highly valued by colleges, as it reflects a student's potential to thrive in a cooperative learning environment.

Showcasing Extracurricular Achievements

Communication plays a crucial role in presenting extracurricular achievements within a college portfolio. Whether it's writing an impactful essay, creating a compelling visual portfolio, or articulating accomplishments in interviews, effective communication allows students to share their experiences and passions confidently.

Demonstrating Problem-Solving Skills

Communication is essential for showcasing problem-solving skills in various situations. From addressing challenges within a team project to tackling issues with coursework, the ability to communicate clearly about the problem and proposed solutions reflects maturity and adaptability—qualities that colleges highly value.

Research and Networking for College Selection

Strong communication skills enables us students to conduct thorough research on potential colleges. Engaging in effective conversations with college representatives, alumni, and current students provides valuable insights that help in making informed decisions about the right fit for further education.

College Admissions Essays and Interviews

In the final stages of the college application process, communication becomes paramount in crafting compelling admission essays and excelling in interviews. The ability to convey one's achievements, aspirations, and uniqueness in writing and speaking greatly influences college admission decisions.

Furthermore, effective communication in high school not only prepares students for college applications but also lays the foundation for success in various aspects of their future endeavors. As they move beyond high school, these communication skills will continue to play a vital role in their academic, personal, and professional lives. Let's explore some of the long-term benefits of strong communication skills:

College Life and Academic Excellence

Once students enter college, effective communication becomes even more crucial. Engaging in classroom discussions, forming study groups, and seeking help from professors all rely on the ability to communicate clearly and confidently. Students who have honed their communication skills in high school find it easier to adapt to college environments and excel in their academic pursuits.

Career Advancement and Employability

In the professional world, communication is a skill highly sought after by employers. Whether it's writing clear emails, delivering presentations, or collaborating with colleagues, effective communication fosters a productive and harmonious work environment. Individuals with strong communication skills are often perceived as reliable team players and are more likely to be considered for leadership positions and career advancement.

Networking and Building Professional Relationships

Networking is essential for career growth, and effective communication is at the core of successful networking. Building meaningful professional relationships involves active listening, expressing ideas clearly, and demonstrating professionalism. High school students who have practiced effective communication will find it easier to network and create valuable connections in their chosen fields.

Advocating for Personal and Professional Goals

Throughout their lives, individuals encounter situations where they need to advocate for their ideas, goals, and beliefs. Negotiating a salary, presenting a business proposal, and engaging in community initiatives all require strong communication skills to empower individuals to articulate their thoughts persuasively and make a lasting impact.

Leadership and Inspiring Others

Effective leaders are often exceptional communicators. They can rally a team, inspire collective action, and articulate a vision that motivates others to strive for success. High school students who have developed leadership skills through communication will have a head start in becoming influential leaders in college, their careers, and their communities.

Conflict Resolution and Emotional Intelligence

Conflict is an inevitable part of life. Strong communication skills enable individuals to navigate conflicts more effectively, leading to better resolution outcomes and positive relationships. Additionally, communication proficiency cultivates emotional intelligence, allowing individuals to understand and manage their emotions, as well as empathize with others.

Community Engagement and Social Impact

Individuals with strong communication skills can effectively engage with their communities, advocate for causes they are passionate about, and contribute to positive social change. Whether it's raising awareness about an issue, volunteering, or participating in civic activities, effective communication amplifies one's ability to make a difference.

In conclusion, communication with others is an essential aspect of high school life with far-reaching implications for a student's future. From building a solid portfolio for college applications to empowering individuals throughout their personal and professional lives, effective communication serves as a cornerstone for success. High school students who actively work on their communication skills will find themselves better equipped to tackle the challenges of college, career, and beyond. It is never too early to start refining these skills, as they will undoubtedly shape the trajectory of a student's life and enable them to make a positive impact on the world around them.

Parent Note: It is important for us as adults to understand that the skills we take for granted such as time management, organization, multi-tasking, conflict resolution, negotiation, stress management are not natural for teenagers. It is difficult for them to understand the cause and effect of their actions at an early age. There is a big difference in perspectives between adults and teenagers on what skills they have developed so far. Most schools in middle and high school years directly start loading students with information. They do not provide any major training on basic organization and time management other than to use notebooks, drives, and files. Teenagers benefit a lot from learning to use simple tools consistently such as arranging folder structure in their laptops, discipline to change file names, creating lists in Excel, notification and sorting important emails, using OneNote, organizing with calendars and logs, and making reminders. As parents, guiding them to write professional and respectful emails to mentors and teachers are our responsibility. With social media, we are raising students who are frivolous with their words and are socially awkward with face-to-face communication. It is important for us to find avenues for them to be in comfort and uncomfortable zones mixing with adults and their peers. Soft skills such as communication, networking, positive attitude, and emotional intelligence can be taught and developed in the high school years. Strength finder tests can be introduced to them from our work environment so that they get to understand teamwork and collaboration.

ACADEMICS/EXTRACURRICULARS

*"The more that you read, the more
things you will know. The more that you
learn, the more places you'll go."*

—DR. SEUSS

Description: *The college admissions process is holistic but one part that is typically weighed more than the rest is academics and extracurriculars. It's important to continue to keep your academics at the top of your priority list while also looking at ways to let your passion drive your academics and other extracurricular activities. This chapter explains the importance of planning the right courses as well as taking classes and participating in clubs that matter.*

CHAPTER 8

Course Planning

Timing: Eighth/Ninth Grade and Tailor
as You Get into Sophomore Year

Course planning in high school for college preparation and beyond is all about setting yourself up for success in the future. It's like laying the groundwork for your dream college or career journey, starting with choosing the right classes.

First, you want to focus on the core subjects and graduation requirements like math, science, English, and social studies. These are the building blocks of knowledge, and colleges pay much attention to how well you do in these classes. So, give it your best shot and try to do your best!

But hold up; it's not just about the core classes. You have to think about what you want to study in college, your interests, and what career you might be interested in. If you have an idea, try taking classes related to that field in your first year or ninth grade. It'll give you a taste of what it's like and help you decide if it's your thing. I wanted to study architecture, so I tried some architecture courses in ninth grade and participated in local baking and bridge building, just to find that I was not enjoying it much.

Here's the thing about course planning: you must challenge yourself but not overwhelm yourself. That is the tough part! How would you know whether you are challenging yourself and not burning yourself out? This is not a science, it is an art.

Here are a few steps that will help any of us in course planning. I attended a public charter school. It is very close to a full public school in terms of curriculum and rigor. However, a private school might be much more flexible with the curriculum.

In any case, do not take all super hard courses in high school just to impress colleges. Take courses to challenge yourself. Finding a balance between pushing yourself to grow and not burning out is essential. Have a growth mindset, and do not do anything you believe your dream college would want to see in your profile. Use common sense on courses that may challenge you and get out of your comfort zone to try those.

Well-Rounded Course Plan

Take a mix of classes for future life skills such as communication, accounting, and economics, no matter your career path. Don't load up on just one subject and neglect the others. We do not want to be engineers with no skills to market ourselves or math graduates without writing skills. Being well-rounded and having the ability to handle different challenges may be far better than just focusing on a single thing beyond college applications.

Know When to Ask for Help

Don't be afraid to ask for help when selecting courses to balance the load! Work with your counselor or parents to understand the prerequisites for every course starting freshman year. The goal is to get an A in all courses; hence, you cannot plan AP courses without the basic courses, and you do not want to plan all AP courses in the same year. A well-established roadmap to complete your prerequisites and graduation requirements is far easier to manage than plan it year after year.

Here are the questions I asked my high school counselor in eighth/ninth grade. These may help you and your parents to think of all possibilities to create a roadmap for yourself.

- What are the minimum graduation requirements for high school?

- What are the prerequisites for every class I want to take?

- Can I do any courses independently from the prerequisites or earlier than freshman year to balance the load in the four years?

- What will my transcript look like if I take courses in the summer, and what are the affiliated universities whose courses the school or school district accepts? What is the approval process for taking these courses, so they appear in one transcript rather than several separate transcripts?

- If I scored less than my planned score for classes taken outside the school, what are my options for dropping from the transcript? (This is a very important question since you are now trying to challenge yourself and trying your best without a teacher and outside a school environment. We have never done this until middle school and are trying to explore our limitations. It teaches us to learn independently, but we can stumble here, and there is nothing wrong with trying and deciding what is best for ourselves. However colleges and admission officers may just see a "C" in the transcript and can question our ability to learn independently. There may be ways to explain this in an application, but to be safe, we need to know our options of keeping it or dropping it from our transcripts.)

- What is the weight of honors classes in the school?

- What is the rule for AP exams? Do we have to enroll in AP exams if we take an AP course in the school, or can we pick and choose the AP exams we want to concentrate on? (For example: This will help you decide to take the AP Calculus BC exam and skip AB since it has both components. May be your dream school for undergraduate studies need both AB and BC for credit as a mandatory class requirement. Maybe focus on the AP exams that you plan to major in. In short know your options and consequences on whether to skip an AP exam or take it.)

- What are dual enrollment courses or concurrent enrollment courses that I am allowed to take? How many in a year? How many credits will it show on my transcript? What are the benefits for taking it and will these be considered as credits for my dream school?

- Do I have to go out of my school campus for the dual or concurrent enrollment courses, or does the school have them in collaboration with local universities? How much does it cost now vs. when I take it in college? How much will the school pay the state, and how much should I pay?

- What are the physical education requirements? Does the school district allow you to show your capability as a competitive level student involved in sports, and can I use that for graduation requirements? Is there a similar category for arts or research?

- What do you or previous teachers see as my strengths and weaknesses? What do they suggest for my course plans? (One teacher told me to avoid a few classes because he thought I would not be happy with so much theoretical knowledge; he saw me as someone who learns visually, and he was absolutely right! I didn't know about it then, but retrospectively, teachers have a different opinion about us than our parents and we do. In my case, I believed I could move mountains, my teachers believed I could move hills, and my parents believed I could move a mound. There was a difference, and each of us was right in our own ways, depending on what I enjoyed.)

- How often can I meet with you, the counselor?

Understanding Dual and Concurrent Enrollment Courses

It is very important to understand these courses' prerequisites, financials, and grade weightage before we take them. Taking dual enrollment in a community college is beneficial if the college you plan to attend accepts these credits and you save money in the long run. It may be beneficial if your school does not offer these subjects. It may be beneficial if you want to dive deep into a particular career. Worst case scenario, find what tutors you have available in your area and if it is affordable in the case you take a course and struggle with it halfway. It is not beneficial to take these courses to increase your weighted grades or to use them to become your school's valedictorian. These courses should show your passion in a subject and should not be available in school, else colleges and admission officers can see through the intention.

We should focus on taking the planned courses no matter who the teacher is and who your friends are. We all have some favorite and not-so-favorite teachers. Just like any other student, I had my own. It's easy to escape conflict and avoid courses or drop out of courses when you do not like a teaching style, or join courses when your favorite teacher teaches it. Adapting to a teaching style and doing your best is far more difficult. This helps in relationship building, and we can learn flexibility, a skill required long after we leave high school. I was advised that I would always not work with the people I like and that I need to be flexible with my attitude, no matter my personality.

Your friends may not be in the courses you take, but it's fine; they are still in school. Our friends' career paths are not the same as ours, so joining the band just to have fun may seem like pleasure in the short term, but we will lose happiness in the long run. If your interests match, that is a different situation, but don't force it and get influenced by friends to join the same courses that they do. In freshman and sophomore years, we want to avoid standing out from others in ways that aren't socially acceptable, and we want to mingle easily. So, some of our decisions are very short-term, and I was no exception. I tried to match my schedule with others just to realize that I was struggling or bored in classes I had no interest in.

Decision on AP Courses and Honors Courses

As you progress through high school, you'll notice that your schedule becomes more flexible, giving you more choices in your courses. This is where you can tailor your academic journey to align with your passions and future goals.

Let's talk about AP and honors courses. These are like the superheroes of high school classes because they offer college-level material and can earn you college credit if you score well on the corresponding AP exams. It is important to find your school's rules on AP exams. They show colleges that you're up for a challenge and can handle more rigorous coursework. But here's the deal: don't go overboard with AP and honors classes to have a fancy transcript. Choose the ones that genuinely interest you and play to your strengths. It's about quality, not quantity!

On the flip side, if you need more time for the intensity of AP or honors courses, that's fine too. Everyone's journey is different, and it's okay to take regular classes and excel in them. The key is to show consistency and dedication in whatever you choose.

Choose the Elective Courses Wisely

Now, let's talk about elective courses. These are the fun ones where you explore your interests beyond the core subjects. Whether music, art, computer programming, or creative writing, electives can add a unique flavor to your high school experience. They showcase your passions and can also help you discover hidden talents.

While exploring your interests is essential, it's equally crucial to consider courses that will align with your intended major or career path. For example, taking extra math and science courses will give you a strong foundation if you're considering pursuing engineering in college. If you're interested in becoming a journalist, focusing on English and communication-related courses can be beneficial. Think about your long-term goals and choose courses that support them. Researching colleges and getting credits earlier in dual and concurrent enrollment is an option.

I did a few courses in public administration administered by a local university because I needed to understand negotiation with external organizations, financial management, and managing people. It was very important as I started my work partnering with UNICEF and my innovation session to influence organizations.

General Roadmap

Our high school course plans typically involve a progression from foundational courses in core subjects like English, math, science, and social studies during the freshman and sophomore years. As we advance to junior and senior years, they often have the flexibility to explore elective courses, honors or Advanced Placement (AP) classes, and potentially dual-enrollment or concurrent enrollment options, tailoring to our interests and post-graduation or career goals.

Graduation Requirement Courses

Front-load your graduation requirements and interesting subjects you want to explore, and focus on your planned major courses in junior and senior year. This will allow flexibility in your schedule as you explore other interest areas and balance extracurriculars and SAT/ACT study in your junior and senior years.

Language Courses

Decide the language course and stick to it for all four years if your school has the classes—Spanish, French, Mandarin, or whatever your school offers. If they do not, look for other ways to keep learning the language. As an eighteen-year-old, I now see the benefit of learning a new language, and I'm glad I did. The ignorance and excuse of not learning a language when given an opportunity is embarrassing, as I work with students worldwide. Even if it's a few words, the connection I make to these students in their local language is very self-satisfactory, and I feel a sense of belonging. You never know when a new language you learned will be useful!

Art Courses

When you take an art course, complete it in the same year in consecutive semesters—Theatre 1 and Theatre 2 or an AP art class the whole year. If possible, do not break it down since it is easier for colleges to see the continuation. There are few colleges that would require you to take it continuously in both semesters.

PE Courses

If you are involved in sports outside school and are a varsity-level or state-level player, you may be able to get an exception in order to skip it and use that for graduation requirements and avoid schedule conflicts. I fenced and was learning to fly a glider, but my hours were not enough for a waiver and hence I planned my PE courses in my sophomore year.

Courses Needed for Certain Colleges

Some basic course requirements exist for certain universities. Go to the university websites and look for high school course recommendations if you are targeting a specific university.

General course outlines that I found for top colleges on different websites and prep scholar blogs:

- English: four years with a preference for writing-intensive courses

- Mathematics: four years—through calculus (interested in engineering and STEM)

- History and Social Studies: three years

- Science: three years of laboratory science and a fourth year preferred, including physics for students considering engineering

- Foreign Language: three years of a single language (ancient or modern) with four preferred

- Other graduation requirements as per your school district such as Physical Education, Art, Volunteer requirements, Driving requirements, and others.

Remember, it's not just about getting into college. It's about finding the right fit for you and using it in the future for your career.

So, that's the lowdown on course planning in high school for college prep. It's all about taking the right classes, getting involved, challenging yourself, and finding the best fit for your future. Stay focused, work hard, and remember that your education is the key to unlocking amazing opportunities!

Lastly, your course plan will not go exactly as you laid down, so please be flexible.

Now, a word of advice: don't let course planning stress you out, and don't compare yourself with your peers' course plans. No two people can have the same interests and same skill set!

Academic planning is essential to preparing for college, but it's just one piece of the puzzle. Your high school years are also about growing, exploring your interests, making friends, and having fun. So, strike a balance between academic pursuits and enjoying the journey.

Lastly, don't be afraid to seek guidance from your teachers, counselors, or older students who have been through your school's college application process. They can offer valuable insights and advice to help you make informed decisions. Talk to your teachers, parents, or guidance counselor if you're struggling with a subject. They're there to support you and help you succeed. There are millions of free resources; if you need specialized tutoring, talk to your parents well in advance.

Course planning in high school for college preparation is an exciting opportunity to shape your academic journey and set yourself up for success.

While I have listed the steps above that may help you, here are some examples of a course load and my opinion on its rigor. Please note the names of courses may be different in each school, but I gave a general name that can be easily understood by most of us.

High School Class Schedule for a Prospective Biology Major

		Student 1	Student 2	Student 3
Freshman Year		**Student 1**	**Student 2**	**Student 3**
	Math	Algebra 1	General Math—9th Grade or Math Course 2 or Course 3 (depends on the school)	AP Calculus AB

	English	9th Grade English	9th Grade English	English Honors
	Science	Biology	Science Honors	Chemistry
	Social Studies	World History	Social Studies 1	AP Human Geography
	Elective	Intro to Computer Science	Life Skills	AP Computer Science
	Language	Spanish		Spanish 3
	PE	PE	PE	PE
	Art	Theatre	Intro to Arts	
Sophomore Year				
	Math	Geometry Honors	Algebra 1	AP Calculus BC
	English	English Honors	10th Grade English	AP Language and Composition
	Science	Chemistry	General Anatomy	AP Chemistry, Physics Honors, Biology
	Social Studies	US History	Social Studies 2	AP World History
	Elective	Programming	Intro to Technology/ Home Economics	

	Language	Spanish 2		Spanish 4 Honors
	PE	PE	PE	PE for Graduation Requirements
	Art	Theater 2		AP Studio Arts
Junior Year				
	Math	Algebra 2 Honors	Algebra 2	AP Statistics
	English	AP English Language and Composition	11th Grade English	AP Literature and Composition
	Science	AP Biology/Physics	Earth Science	AP Biology, AP Physics 1
	Social Studies	AP US History	Social Studies 3	AP US History
	Elective	Psychology	Personal Finance/Media Studies	AP Psychology
	Language	Spanish 3	Spanish 1	AP Spanish
Senior Year				
	Math	Precalculus Honors	Geometry	Linear Math
	English	AP English Literature and Composition	12th Grade English	

Science	AP Chemistry AP Environmental Science		AP Physics C
Social Studies	Government and Economics Honors	Social Studies 4	AP Government and Politics
Elective	Advanced Anatomy and Physiology (Elective)	Travel and Tourism (Elective) Introduction to Music (Elective)	AP Research AP Macroeconomics AP Microeconomics
Language	AP Spanish	Spanish 2	

Student 1 starts with English Honors and math courses to establish a strong foundation in critical thinking and problem-solving skills. They also take regular and honors science courses in their freshman and sophomore years to build a solid understanding of fundamental scientific principles before diving into AP Biology and AP Chemistry in their junior and senior years.

Student 1 also takes Spanish courses to demonstrate language proficiency, which can benefit a biology major. Additionally, they explore different interests through electives like Intro to Computer Science, Art, Psychology, and Advanced Anatomy and Physiology. The combination of core classes, AP classes, and electives allows the student to showcase their dedication to academics, interest in the sciences, college-readiness and well-roundedness. This student has challenged themselves with the right rigor and has consistently shown an interest in biology, ending with an elective of an interested major.

Student 2 has a less intense high school schedule. In this example, the student's class schedule needs more challenging courses and advanced subjects that could better prepare them for college. The student takes basic or regular English, math, and science courses, which may not adequately develop the critical thinking and analytical skills needed for success at the next level of education. The student did not have a passion or interest in any subject and opted for the subject as and when schedules allowed.

Additionally, the elective choices focus on general and less rigorous subjects like Home Economics, Media Studies, and Introduction to Music, which may not provide the academic depth needed for college readiness. The lack of honors, AP, or dual enrollment classes also means the student misses out on opportunities to earn college credit while still in high school and have potentially taken the easier path. These courses can save time and money by allowing students to skip introductory college classes.

Student 3 has many AP classes and the most rigorous schedule, but are you particularly interested? It seems like they are an intended STEM major, and they have taken all AP classes offered in school, but the lack of electives shows that the focus is just on taking courses. In this example, Student 3 has loaded up their schedule with many AP classes, often taking multiple AP courses in a year. While AP classes can be beneficial for students seeking to challenge themselves and show impressive transcripts, this schedule could be more relaxed. It can lead to burnout and stress with no major focus other than a rat race to compare with others and focus on college applications. Most students who want to aim for Ivy Leagues and top colleges have a similar schedule, but what we do not see is apart from this, they may have electives and other activities that show their passion and complements their course load. It is recommended on all websites that if you want to target top schools, you have to take the highest classes offered in your school, but most of us need to understand that we can take all the highest classes offered if we have the capacity, while still focusing on our interest areas.

The opportunity to take classes that interest you and electives that may have given you a chance to explore, have fun and enhance your extracurriculars are missing in this schedule, and the admissions officer may look at you as not having any focused passion.

It is a myth that having a schedule like Student 3's will get you into the top colleges. Having a purpose and reasoning for every class you take would have been far more beneficial to this student so we can put a story together on which courses helped us grow as an individual.

I personally know of a student who wanted to major in Biomedical engineering and the only Bio course planned was in the senior year AP–Bio, since her school allowed taking AP Bio without a Biology Honors or Biology course. She was an academically exceptional student with a 4.0 Unweighted GPA and a 36 ACT with stellar extracurriculars, but it was too late for her to change anything about her course plan. Her internship was in Lockheed Martin unrelated to Biology. She ended up changing her major to Physics reluctantly while applying and found it difficult to write essays on a subject that was not much interest to her. Retrospectively, the guidance offered for course planning was minimal in her case in the first few years of high schools. Hence requesting for guidance or confirming with the high school counselor to ensure if your courses are balanced and appropriate for a career path you are choosing is very important. If you are still curious about her, she did not get in to her top five choices, but got in to one her safeties. She later decided to change her major again to Biology and is planning to try in her dream schools for graduate studies.

SAT/ACT Prep

This may change for future graduates. These tests may still linger for a few years or change formats since it is already being digital this year. When it comes to standardized tests like the SAT or ACT, start preparing early. Take practice tests, study the areas you need help with, and try to improve in sections where you score low. It is more important to plan these tests at the right time with a buffer in your schedule to take them multiple times. Hundreds of resources, including Khan Academy, are available to prepare for these tests. Work back from the dream university you want to attend, the average scores of their accepted students, and the target for that score. It is an important component, so you need to try repeatedly to improve here. For about 2-3 months, I consistently went almost every Saturday morning, except for the days I was traveling to give my practice test. Finally, when I gave my test, it was almost a second nature. In my opinion, the strategy for giving these tests are more important.

I do not like to sit in a place for 1 to 2 hours, so it took a lot of practice to just focus and be in the same spot for hours. Also, I am very sensitive to sounds and I noticed that in the exam location, I could hear turning papers, sighs and calculator touches. I would know every single thing that happened in the exam room and I had to train myself to focus and ignore those distractions. To train myself, I sometimes gave these practice tests when I was traveling in a flight or in airports to see if my scores were consistent in spite of the noise level. There are many websites that provide you strategies for answering the questions in the standardized test and the only advice is sleep well and eat a healthy breakfast, but none of them gives us the insight into what all can happen in that exam venue for some of us who can get distracted easily. Long bathroom lines during break, an hour of going through the rules before the test, and constant sound of papers are some of them that you need to be aware of and be prepared.

Summary

Choose classes that align with your interests and future goals, challenge yourself without overwhelming yourself, and get involved in extracurricular activities that showcase your passions. Remember, it's not just about impressing colleges; it's about finding your path, growing as an individual, and creating a bright future for yourself. So, embrace the process, stay true to yourself, and enjoy the ride!

Some potential problems with overloaded schedules for high achievers or for those who want to focus just on college applications are:

Time Management

With so many rigorous courses, students may struggle to manage their time effectively, leading to incomplete assignments or cramming for exams. It has happened to me, and I can say with no qualms that I struggled.

High-Stress Levels

The workload from numerous AP classes can be overwhelming, causing high stress and anxiety for the student.

Lack of Balance

The schedule leaves little room for extracurricular activities, hobbies, or even adequate rest, which are essential for a well-rounded high school experience.

Limited Social Interaction

Overloading AP classes may limit the time the student has for socializing and developing interpersonal skills.

Risk of Burnout

The relentless pressure to perform at an exceptionally high level in all classes can lead to burnout and decreased motivation.

Students must challenge themselves academically, but it's equally important to balance academics, extracurriculars, and personal well-being. Schools, parents, and students should work together to create a schedule for growth and achievement while considering the student's mental and physical well-being.

There is a course placemat I created and followed, based on my interest at a high level. Course placemats are segmented groups of ideas and plans for your courses. Somewhere after my freshman year, it was the first placemat I created for myself. I had a general idea of what I wanted to accomplish at the end of the next three years. It was not the rigor of classes or the exact classes that were important, but the general boxes were important for me. If I knew the class name, I would add it, or else I just said I want to develop basic genetic engineering skills.

I would update it very often after every semester to check against my passion and see if I was on the right track. Some years, I was behind on some skills due to schedule, and some years, I was ahead. I did not complete 100 percent of my plan here, but 75 percent was taken care of. You will see some "To Be Determined" (TBD) and some high-level skills with no course names or plan of where I will perform research or internship. However, this gave me a good view of what I was going after and why I was doing what I was doing.

The questions to ask while using this placemat are:

- Is this a rigorous enough academic plan that allows me to challenge myself?
- Do the schedule and courses allow me to develop my character?
- Does it build my skills—academic (technical) and non-academic (soft skills)?
- Does it allow me to make an impact?
- Does it define my passion?

⚠ Fill in the empty Course Placemat, laminate it or decorate it in front of your study table. Looking at it always helps knowing that we are taking a path that is unique to ourselves. It helps build confidence in the hard work we have put so far and the journey ahead!

Innovation/Product Development in Healthcare/Sustainable Dev.

Device Development/ Engineering Design
- *Physics*
- *3D design intern*
- *Architecture/Engineering basics*
- *Hands-on engineering skills*
- *Computational and Programming*

Entrepreneurship/Business
- *Marketing*
- *Intro Business Principles*
- *Economics (AP Macro/Micro)*

Public Administration
- *Basic accounting/finance skills*
- *Basic negotiation and people skills*
- *Basic Project management*
- *Basic tools for planning*

Communication/Writing
- *AP Language courses*
- *Seek Speaking or presenting opportunities*
- *Blogs/Vlogs*
- *Partnership with organizations*
- *Potential published book*

Research Skills
- *Research/Internships*
- *Lab experience*
- *Scientific writing experience*
- *Presentation experience*
- *Summer programs*

Microbiology and Genetics
- *Chem/ AP Chem*
- *Biology/ AP Biology*
- *Basic Genetic Engineering*
- *Cell Biology*

Humanities: *TBD*, **Foreign Language:** *Mandarin*, **Strategy and Innovation:** *TBD*
Core Courses/Grad requirements: *Math till AP Calc AB or BC as per schedule, Social Studies, Art, PE, Others*

Course Placement

Transcript Monitoring Sheets

Future Outlook: How to Use Tools like ChatGPT?

While I did most of this manually, the future graduating class of 2024 and beyond can be much more productive with AI tools.

Using tools like ChatGPT for course planning and determining which classes to take can be a helpful way to gather information and insights. Here's a step-by-step guide on how you can utilize ChatGPT for this purpose:

Define Your Goals and Interests

Start by considering your academic interests, career aspirations, and any specific goals you have in mind. This will help you focus on the right courses and AP classes.

Compile a list of questions: Jot down specific questions you want to ask ChatGPT. For example:

- What are the benefits of taking AP classes?

- Which AP classes align with my interests in [subject]?

- What are the recommended prerequisites for AP classes?

- How do colleges view AP classes during the admissions process?

Access a ChatGPT Interface

Look for platforms or websites that provide access to a ChatGPT interface. OpenAI Playground or other AI-powered chat platforms are good options.

Start a Conversation

Note that conversation with a AI tool like ChatGPT are called "prompts". Begin your conversation with ChatGPT prompts by asking ChatGPT to play a role and then introducing your role. You can then ask a series of questions through prompts. For example, you can say, "Hello! Assume the role of a high school counselor. I'm a high school student interested in planning my courses. Can you help me by answering some questions?"

Ask Your Questions

Pose your questions to ChatGPT one at a time, providing as much context as possible. Be specific about your interests, current academic level, and any relevant information that could assist ChatGPT in providing accurate guidance.

Evaluate Responses Critically

Remember that ChatGPT's responses are made based off of previous data as well as patterns that is has analyzed. While it can offer valuable insights, it's important to critically evaluate the information and consider additional sources, such as academic advisors, college websites, or trusted educational resources.

Seek Multiple Perspectives

While ChatGPT can provide a helpful starting point, consulting with other resources and individuals is beneficial. Talk to your teachers, school counselors, and experienced students who can offer personal experiences and tailored advice.

Make an Informed Decision

After gathering information from ChatGPT and other sources, take some time to analyze and weigh the options available. Consider factors such as your academic strengths, personal interests, long-term goals, and the availability of courses at your school.

Remember, ChatGPT is an AI language model and does not have personal experiences or real-time knowledge. It's a tool that can provide insights and guidance based on many use-cases and scenarios it has learnt from, but ultimately, your judgment and the expertise of professionals should be taken into account when making important decisions like course planning. We will cover more about AI in the next section.

Use of AI for Personalized Learning and Productivity

In the past few years, Artificial Intelligence has been a subject of discussion as a means to improve learning and education. Intelligent bots and machines can learn from past behaviors and suggest new material.

However, this conversation has exploded recently with the breakthrough and emergence of tools such as ChatGPT, Bard and others. These tools use a special type of AI called Generative AI to create new and novel information based on the information the machine is trained on.

This means that AI can now be used for developing tools that can be personalized to support an individual.

I believe everybody should make the best use of these technologies to get an edge in their preparation. Some of the uses and scenarios where I think AI can be best used to supplement our preparation are:

- **Real-time tutoring or in-line guide:** Intelligent chatbots can be great tutors. Khan Academy now offers "KhanAmigo" a generative AI-based personal tutor that helps you learn not by giving an answer but by providing small hints in context of the problem that is being solved, leading to solving the problem by yourself. There are other similar bots emerging and they will only become better.

- **Custom personalized study planning:** An AI-based tool can learn everything about you, from you, and using the information gathered from thousands of other similar profiles can create a personalized plan that is just for you.

- **Feedback and support:** Sometimes you need a second pair of eyes who can be critical of your work and provide feedback and suggest improvement. AI can be that partner.

- **Grade projection and assessments:** Data about grades, scores, gradings curves, grade inflation across many years, can be used to create a projection of your grades to give areas of improvement and subsequent even suggest courses to improve chances in the college of interest.

However, just like any tool, especially powerful ones like AI, there are several pitfalls we should be aware of. Some of the challenges of AI that we should be aware of are as follows:

- **Social Isolation:** Working with others create not only opportunities to learn but also offers relief from the stress of constant work. AI tools cannot replace human engagement of working with friends and others who can help us provide insights.

- **Bias:** AI recommendations are based on the information that is fed to it when it was trained. Given there is always some bias in our society whether it is economic status, gender or cultural diversity, AI engines reflect them in their recommendations, which may not be at all representing any of us.

- **Privacy:** Learning is a continuous activity. While AI tools provide us guidance based on the data it has learnt from, it also simultaneously learns from our questions, level of knowledge, and mistakes. There should be an acute awareness that all of our data and information is stored, tracked and used to train future versions of the engines.

- **Cost:** The AI tools are not cheap. To access a sophisticated AI tool would require budgeting a substantial amount, which may not be possible for lot of students.

Artificial intelligence is here to stay. It will completely change how we learn, study and play. Things will become better and likely cheaper in the very near future. There will also be better oversight on some of the risks. Instead of completely rejecting it, a more prudent approach would be to learn and get comfortable with a tool that can be a great companion for our success.

CHAPTER 9

Selecting Extracurriculars

Timing: Freshman and Sophomore years

When it comes to extracurricular activities, quality is more important than quantity. Rather than joining every club under the sun, focus on a few that interest you. Become an active member. These activities show colleges that you're not just a bookworm but also someone who can positively impact the community.

And let's remember community service and volunteering! We are responsible for giving back to our communities regardless of the resources we have. So, find a cause you're passionate about and get involved. It's a win-win situation—you're making a difference while boosting your skill set.

We must remember the type of extracurricular activities! It will make it easier to be committed to it if you enjoy it. Chapter 1 gave you some framework for combining your passion and skill to choose an activity where you can show commitment, excellence, and leadership. It will also make it easier for you when you write your essays to show why you picked what, how it defines you, why you're involved in your community outside of the classroom, and what made you do that. It could be sports, clubs, arts, music, research, or anything that shows you're passionate and dedicated.

Selecting the right extracurriculars in high school can significantly impact your college admissions process. Admissions committees try to identify students who are well-rounded, demonstrate a genuine passion for their interests, and contribute positively to their communities. Choosing the right extracurriculars can help you beyond college application. You will want to keep working on it and use that as a purpose for your adult life. No one in the college admission process is expecting you to pick an activity that will look shiny in the admission process if you don't want to do it and if you will stop doing it once you get accepted.

Let me share a story of an activity that could have been a better fit. A good friend of mine went every Saturday to a community cafe whose mission was to provide food to people of all backgrounds. The payment was optional for those who could not afford it. She did this from middle school for about five to eight hours on weekends. Sometime in her sophomore year, she was informed by a college counselor that this would not be very attractive to top colleges and that she should start her nonprofit to do something else.

Reluctantly, she stopped going to the community cafe! With the help of a college counselor and parents, she created a fancy website, registered a nonprofit for beginner coding classes for girls in the community, requested a few highly accomplished students to join her, and offered coding classes for an after-school club, where about five students joined. She did this for three to four months before realizing that it was boring, nobody wanted to contribute, and many other organizations in the community were doing the same thing. Her counselor asked her to create podcasts, and she spent weekends creating podcasts and publishing this. She did this for another few months and stopped it. High school academics came in the way, and college applications started; she made up her passion for STEM and coding and shared some statistics regarding her influence on local students through coding using the website. She was unhappy about the entire process, did not like what she wrote in her essays, and felt stuck and influenced by external individuals. She was disappointed in herself that she did not stay with her instincts and what she loved to do for years. In the middle of senior year, she went back to the community cafe where she felt like herself. She applied for a few more scholarships and colleges with her story and reasons for stopping her original passion for her community work and later coming back to it. She described how she felt in the community cafe where the six to eight hours didn't feel like work. I am happy to share that she not only got accepted into her dream university but also got a full ride from a private scholarship as a reward for her integrity and honesty in sticking with what she loves to do. This is a successful story where the ending is happy. However, that is not true in most cases and many, in spite of putting years of work in what they believed in true extracurricular supporting the community, it didn't give them fulfillment or the benefit they hoped for with their application. This was mostly because it was never something they owned and felt truly connected to. Taking a cookie-cutter approach to success because someone else has taken this path or has been successful earlier is easier, but is that what we want to do, or do we want to be unique?

Here's a step-by-step guide to selecting the right extracurriculars beyond college admissions:

Discover Your Interests and Passions

Begin by exploring your interests and passions. What activities make you excited and engaged? Reflect on what you enjoy doing in your free time and what brings you a sense of accomplishment. Consider your strengths and talents and areas you want to develop further. (This is explained more in-depth in Chapter 1.)

Quality Over Quantity

It's not about joining numerous clubs and organizations but about dedicating meaningful time and effort to a few activities you're passionate about. Admissions officers value depth and commitment in their extracurricular pursuits over a laundry list of superficial involvements. They want to know if you will do this beyond acceptance. Does the activity make you who you are?

Align with Your Academic Goals

Consider extracurriculars complementing your academic interests and career aspirations. For instance, if you're interested in engineering, participating in robotics or coding clubs can demonstrate your commitment to the field and showcase relevant skills. If you are interested in journalism, participate in writing clubs, newsletters, and communication-related activities. This is a no-brainer, but we need to remember it in the rat race and try and seek all clubs and activities without understanding what we want to do and why we are doing this.

Leadership and Initiative

When you are ready, your teachers will appreciate students who take the initiative and assume leadership roles to help the clubs they sponsor. Look for opportunities to become a leader in your chosen extracurricular activities, whether being a club president, a team captain, or a leader in community service projects. Set expectations with the club members to ensure it is beneficial for all.

Engage in Community Service/Volunteering

Community service demonstrates your commitment to positively impact the world around you. We live in a world where we are all connected. Some are more fortunate than others. This is chance for you to find a purpose and start serving your community. Participate in activities that go hand in hand with your interests while addressing school, local, or global needs.

Seek Diversity and Balance

Pursue activities that provide a well-rounded experience. Balance academic pursuits with physical activities, artistic endeavors, and community involvement. Diversity in your activities improves your adaptability and ability to manage your time effectively. In times where you are alone, you may want to play a sport, play an instrument, or write a journal to give yourself a break, and these will help you beyond admissions.

Showcase Achievements and Awards

If you want to improve yourself, apply for awards as a motivation to excel in any extracurriculars. Make sure to highlight these achievements, and let this encourage you to excel further.

Start Early and Demonstrate Long-Term Commitment

Admissions officers and everyone who judges us, whether for a job or a seat in the college, appreciate consistency and dedication. Starting early in high school allows you to demonstrate a long-term commitment to your activities, which will improve your skills in the long run. By senior year, extracurriculars will become a way of life rather than another activity you are forced to add.

For some of us, our extracurriculars may become a responsibility rather than a luxury or activity as we take this path. You may be helping the local students or seniors who soon depend on you. Set expectations with them, manage your schedule, and recruit more help to sustain this beyond your schedule. Think of ways to improve the process so that they can be fine without your help and time. For example, you may be helping one of your school teachers to help in her biology class by helping in the lab, correcting papers—not as an official TA, but because you like to do it. The teacher and students are now dependent on you. Set expectations with the teacher on when and how long you can do it. Ask your peers if someone else can do it when you are absent, or share the process or a flyer with details on how to do it for someone to pick it up quickly.

Create a Well-Crafted Story

Your extracurriculars should contribute to the overall narrative of your college application and beyond. Showcase how your interests, passions, and extracurricular pursuits have shaped your character, values, and future aspirations, which will help you in the long run. It is okay to change your narrative, but know why you are doing so, just like how an adult would change a career path and explain why they did so.

Time Management and Academic Performance

Academic performance should remain your top priority. Participating in extracurriculars should not negatively impact your grades or coursework. Show that you can manage your time effectively and maintain high academic standards.

Stay Genuine and Authentic

Avoid engaging in activities just for the sake of college applications. Colleges seek authentic individuals who pursue their passions sincerely. Being genuine to yourself is essential throughout the application process, and it is best for you in the long run.

Summer Program List

In conclusion, selecting the right activities in high school is about pursuing your passions, showcasing leadership and initiative, and engaging in activities that complement your academic goals. Quality, not quantity, is key, and a thoughtful, well-rounded approach to extracurricular activities can help you stand out overall. Remember to stay true to yourself and demonstrate genuine enthusiasm for the extracurriculars you pursue.

CHAPTER 10

Building an Organization

Timing: Sophomore to Senior Year

Building an organization as a teenager while managing school work requires dedication, time management, and a strategic approach. It's essential to balance your entrepreneurial pursuits and academic responsibilities. Understanding why you are building an organization and whether you need it is essential. If you need an organization, get out of your comfort zone and get it done.

Here is part of my LinkedIn post that I created a while back, and it applies here to decide if you need it:

Many nonprofits are started by well-intentioned high school students like me who want to make an impact and improve their leadership and entrepreneurial skill sets. Though well-intentioned, the ability to scale and self-sustain these organizations need a lot of time, resources, and attention, which sometimes can become a monotonous routine taking us away from the impact we wanted to make and not to mention the time constraints of a busy school year. Hence, most end up with limited short-

term goals and not to their full potential. In addition, the crowding of the ecosystem with organizations with very similar goals results in any grants, funds, and resources out there being thinly distributed. This adversely affects organizations that have worked for years and plan to be there for years...

A quick search https://www.guidestar.org/search for the United States may help us decide if we want to start one or partner with one with a similar mission and vision to make an impact and make a difference.

You can read the full article here:

https://www.linkedin.com/pulse/helping-communities-through-collaborations-non-profit-gitanjali-rao/

If you decide organization is necessary and the right way for you since you have a unique vision and need grants to sustain it, here's a step-by-step guide to help you build and manage an organization while being a successful student:

Identify Your Passion and Purpose

Choose a cause or a business idea you are truly passionate about. A strong sense of purpose will keep you motivated during challenging times and make the journey more fulfilling.

Develop a Clear Vision and Plan

Outline your organization's goals, mission, and objectives. Create a detailed business plan that includes the target audience, strategies for growth, potential challenges, and ways to overcome them. Having a clear roadmap will guide your actions and decision-making.

Decide on the Type of Organization You Want to Start

Do you want it to be an umbrella group or a new nonprofit? There are pros and cons for both. A new one needs much work to build a reputation but will have no constraints. An umbrella one will have a structure, but you need to follow the code of conduct of the mother organization. Starting a formal non-profit that raises and manages funds, can have implications on costs and taxes. Consult a tax professional for the right organization. In the US the most popular ones are 501c organizations, but they too have flavors depending on your structure and size of the funds you manage. Keep the focus on the problem you're solving with your organization.

Start Small and Gradually Scale Up

As a teenager managing school work, starting small and manageable is crucial. Begin with achievable goals and gradually expand your organization as you gain experience and find more time to invest. Decide on your organization's name and appoint a board of directors who can advise you.

Build a Support Network

Seek guidance and support from mentors, teachers, and experienced entrepreneurs who can offer valuable insights and advice. Connect with like-minded individuals who share your passion for the cause or business. Recruit volunteers who can carry out your mission.

Set Realistic Time Frames

Recognize your limited time due to your academic commitments. Set realistic timelines for your organization's growth and milestones, taking into account your school schedule, but dream of the impossible beyond high school.

Create a Schedule and Prioritize

Develop a weekly schedule with specific time blocks for school work, organization tasks, and personal time. Prioritize your school work, and ensure you meet academic deadlines.

Maximize Productivity

Optimize your study sessions by creating a conducive environment, minimizing distractions, and staying focused. Efficient study habits will allow you to complete school work more quickly, freeing time for your organization.

Delegate and Collaborate

If possible, involve team members or friends who share your vision—delegate tasks and responsibilities to distribute the workload and ensure smooth functioning.

Utilize Technology and Tools

Leverage technology and productivity tools to streamline organizational tasks, communication, and time management. To stay organized, use project management apps, scheduling tools, and communication platforms.

Maintain a Healthy Work-Life Balance

Avoid burnout by making time for relaxation, hobbies, and spending time with friends and family. A well-rested mind is more productive and creative.

Communicate with Your Support System

Inform your teachers, parents, and mentors about your entrepreneurial endeavors. Communication is vital in ensuring they understand your commitments and can provide the necessary support.

Learn to Adapt and Be Flexible

Be prepared to adapt your plans and strategies as challenges arise. Flexibility is crucial in managing both your organization and school work effectively.

Celebrate Achievements

Acknowledge and celebrate your milestones and achievements, no matter how small. Positive reinforcement will keep you motivated on your entrepreneurial journey.

Seek Help When Needed

If you are overwhelmed, don't hesitate to ask for help. Reach out to teachers, mentors, or even friends for assistance with school work or organizational tasks.

Building an organization as a teenager while managing school work is undoubtedly challenging, but with determination, effective time management, and a supportive network, it's entirely possible to achieve your entrepreneurial goals while excelling academically. It will also be an outlet for your family and friends who want to do good for the community but lack a trusted partner. They will be more than happy to help you in your endeavor. Managing an organization is complex, but the experiences are invaluable and contribute to your personal and professional growth.

Parent Note: As parents, we sometimes fail to understand the need for our child to take fewer challenging courses, when the only major responsibility a high schooler has is to study and have fun. Or we do not get the fact that they need to be challenged because high school years are the only years they can have fun.

However, for someone to grow as a well-rounded individual, every class—whether it is challenging or not—is important. The improvement year after year should be visible both in attitude and skills to become a better person. The process the students go through to understand themselves and their abilities is so important. It is important that the placemat shared above is a family discussion to get a feel of what is truly feasible and what is not truly feasible and realistic based on your own family schedule, attention, and affordability. Dual enrollments, concurrent enrollment classes, and AP exams need payments. Scholarships are available for dual and concurrent enrollment classes, and helping your student find them is a better way for them to learn the financial discipline as they are getting ready for their college and career. Academic planning is an important step where you can guide the student on a career path that they may not be aware of. As parents, we know certain career paths that may seem cool for a high school student are not so cool when you need to feed a family. You have seen your student since childhood. You know their strengths and weaknesses! They may have a course plan that will move a mountain within a few years, but you have seen their working style and know the reality. Their teachers may have a different perspective. The one thing we can learn is to ignore the rat race and competition no matter which high school your child goes to and create a path that is unique to your student and that fits for your family. This will not only help thinking big but will help break from stereotypes. No matter what, set high expectations from your child and commit yourself to supporting your student.

It is important to sit monthly with your teenager and understand their extracurriculars in order to see how to support them with figuring out logistics, determining how to finance, dealing with registering nonprofit organizations, running background checks, and discussing with counselors and mentors on how you can help. It is a delicate balance where teachers and schools do not want to communicate with you, since your high school student is a growing adult and should be independent. However, keeping communications open, clear, and transparent are equally important so your student knows that they have advocates for their efforts and ambitions.

ACHIEVEMENT

*"Satisfaction lies in the effort, not in the
attainment, full effort is full victory."*

—MAHATMA GANDHI

Description: *Success and achievement is the effect of hard work. It's
important to gain visibility and recognition for your work so that you
not only have continued motivation, but other people know about the
efforts you're making to create a difference. This chapter discusses
the importance of achievement and ways in which to garner visibility
while still maintaining humility, passion, and creativity.*

CHAPTER 11

Well-Rounded Individual Portfolio

Timing: Throughout High School Years

First of all, what is a well-rounded portfolio?

A well-rounded portfolio encompasses various aspects of a student's life and showcases their abilities beyond just their academic performance. It includes academic achievements, extracurricular activities, community involvement, leadership roles, work experiences, and personal interests. When college admissions officers review applications, they are not only looking for students with exceptional grades but also individuals who will bring a dynamic and enriching presence to their campus community.

Academic achievements are undoubtedly essential. Colleges want students who can handle rigorous coursework and demonstrate intellectual curiosity. A strong GPA, challenging course load, excellent performance in AP or IB classes, and a 2 year diploma similar to an AP curriculum, all demonstrate a student's academic prowess. Standardized test scores, such as the SAT or ACT, also provide insights into a student's potential for success in college.

However, it's important to note that while academics form a crucial foundation, they are not the sole determining factor for admission and success in life.

Extracurricular activities are an integral part of developing a well-rounded individual. Admissions officers seek students who have shown dedication, leadership, and passion outside the classroom. Participation in clubs, sports, arts, or community service showcases a student's ability to manage time effectively and demonstrates a commitment to personal interests and causes. Holding leadership positions in these activities indicates the ability to influence and work collaboratively with others, traits valued by colleges as they seek to build a vibrant campus community.

Community involvement is another key component. Volunteering for local charities, engaging in service projects, or participating in outreach initiatives highlight a student's altruism and desire to make a positive impact on the world.

Work experiences can also add value to a student's portfolio. Holding a part-time job or internship during high school demonstrates responsibility, time management skills, and the ability to balance academics and work commitments. It also develops a practical experience beyond the classroom.

Moreover, colleges value unique talents and interests. Students with exceptional skills in music, arts, sports, or other areas can stand out in the admissions process. Demonstrating dedication and achievements in these fields not only adds diversity to the incoming class but also showcases a student's ability to excel in areas they are passionate about.

A well-rounded portfolio not only exhibits a student's accomplishments but also reveals their personality, values, and character. Personal essays and recommendation letters provide insights into a student's aspirations, resilience, and self-awareness. Admissions officers seek students who can contribute positively to the campus culture, foster a sense of inclusivity, have a good character, and actively participate in the learning community. Long story short, it is much more than just exceptional grades. It encompasses a diverse range of achievements, experiences, and qualities that collectively showcase a student's potential to thrive in a college setting and beyond. Academic achievements, extracurricular involvement, community service, work experiences, unique talents, and personal qualities all contribute to a holistic and compelling college application. It is crucial for students to identify purpose and pursue their passions while balancing academic pursuits, as this will not only strengthen their applications but also foster personal growth and development beyond those college admissions. Remember, the college admissions process is not just about impressing colleges, but also about discovering who you are and what you want to achieve in your academic and personal journey.

Prioritizing Social Life in High School and Using It to Create a Well-Rounded College Application

Prioritizing a social life in high school is essential for growing, developing, and becoming a well-rounded individual. By actively engaging in social activities, you can enhance your overall high school experience while demonstrating important qualities to colleges. Here are some in-depth tips on how to prioritize your social life in high school and leverage it effectively for a strong college application:

Effective Time Management

Balancing academics, extracurricular activities, and a social life requires careful time management. Create a detailed schedule that allocates specific time slots for studying, participating in activities, and spending time with friends. Prioritize your commitments and be realistic about how much time you can dedicate to each area. By effectively managing your time, you can ensure that your social life doesn't interfere with your academic responsibilities.

Join Diverse Clubs and Organizations

Actively seek out clubs and organizations that align with your interests and passions. Joining diverse groups allows you to meet likeminded peers who share similar goals and values. Participating in extracurricular activities not only provides opportunities for personal growth and skill development but also helps you build lasting friendships and connections. Colleges appreciate applicants who demonstrate a commitment to their interests beyond the classroom.

Volunteer and Engage in Community Service

Engaging in community service is a powerful way to make a positive impact while developing important life skills. Look for volunteer opportunities that resonate with you and align with your values. There are tons of them where the community needs help. Find a fit! By actively contributing to your community, you demonstrate a sense of empathy, leadership, and civic responsibility. Colleges value applicants who show a genuine commitment to making a difference in the world and share their knowledge.

Attend Social Events and Build Relationships

Actively participate in school social events such as dances, sports games, cultural festivals, talent shows, and other gatherings. These events provide valuable opportunities to meet new people, expand your social circle, and create memorable experiences. Building relationships with classmates, teachers, and mentors can also lead to strong recommendations for your college application.

Pursue Leadership Roles

Seek out leadership positions within clubs, organizations, or student government. Taking on leadership roles showcases your ability to take initiative, collaborate effectively, and motivate others. It also demonstrates your commitment to personal growth and your willingness to make a positive impact on your community. Your own teachers and college counselors appreciate students who display leadership potential and a drive to enact change.

Develop Strong Interpersonal Skills

Effective communication, teamwork, and interpersonal skills are highly valued by colleges and future employers. Engage in activities that enhance these skills, such as participating in group projects, joining debate teams, or taking part in public speaking competitions. These experiences not only foster personal growth but also demonstrate your ability to work well with others and contribute meaningfully to a team.

Maintain a Healthy Work-Life Balance

While engaging in a vibrant social life, it's crucial to maintain a healthy balance with your academic responsibilities. Stay organized, manage your time effectively, and prioritize your studies. Strive for academic excellence while also enjoying your social life. Finding a balance demonstrates discipline, adaptability, and the ability to manage multiple commitments simultaneously.

Document and Reflect on Your Experiences

Keep a comprehensive record of your social engagements, extracurricular activities, leadership roles, and community service projects. Maintain a portfolio that highlights your achievements and growth throughout high school. Quantify your growth as an individual, write down statistics such as "influenced ten additional students to join the club" or "learned skill sets to present and presented in three symposiums." This documentation will serve as a valuable resource when it comes time to complete your college applications, ensuring that you don't overlook any significant experiences.

Articulate the Value of Your Experiences

When applying to colleges, take the time to reflect on how your social life and extracurricular activities have shaped you as an individual. Consider the skills, values, and lessons you have gained through these experiences. Use your college essays and interviews to convey how your social interactions have contributed to your personal growth, leadership abilities, and commitment to making a positive impact. By articulating the value of your experiences, you provide everyone with a deeper understanding of your character and potential contributions to their campus community.

Remember, being a well-rounded individual enhances your college application and it much more than academic achievements. Colleges seek applicants who demonstrate a genuine passion for learning, personal development, strong character, and engagement with their communities. By prioritizing your social life in high school and leveraging it effectively, you can create a comprehensive application that showcases your unique strengths, interests, and character.

CHAPTER 12

Garnering Visibility and Recognition

Timing: Throughout High school years

Embarking on research and projects as a teenager can be an exhilarating and enriching experience. However, it is equally important to gain visibility for your work to receive the recognition it deserves. This chapter will guide you through the process of increasing visibility for your teenage research and projects, with a focus on staying motivated, bringing awareness to the problems you are trying to solve, conveying authenticity for your work, and gaining recognition. By following these strategies, you can amplify the impact of your work and open doors to exciting opportunities. Let's dive in!

Choose a Compelling Topic

To capture attention, select a topic that is both meaningful and unique to you. Consider your interests, passions, and areas where you can contribute something innovative. Brainstorm ideas and evaluate their feasibility and potential impact. By choosing a compelling topic, you lay the foundation for bringing awareness and contributing to society in a positive manner.

Conduct Thorough Research

Immerse yourself in thorough research on your chosen topic. Familiarize yourself with existing literature, studies, and projects to understand the current state of knowledge. This will enable you to identify gaps in the field and develop a research question or project that adds value. In-depth research will strengthen your understanding and allow you to present your work with confidence. This can be in any areas and skill sets you are passionate about.

Plan and Execute Effectively

Create a detailed plan outlining the objectives, methodology, timeline, and available resources for your research or project. Break it down into smaller achievable goals and track your progress. Effective planning and execution demonstrate your commitment and professionalism—both of which are crucial for gaining recognition.

Seek Mentorship and Collaboration

Don't hesitate to seek guidance from experienced mentors or experts in your chosen field. They can provide valuable insights, feedback, and help refine your work. Collaborating with peers who share similar interests can also enhance the quality of your research or project. My first book, *A Young Innovator's Guide to STEM*, provides a chapter on teamwork, so you can be an effective team member yourself and enable others to be effective team members. Leveraging mentorship and collaboration enhances your visibility and showcases your ability to work as part of a team.

Document and Present Your Work

Maintain a comprehensive record of your research or project, including data, observations, methodology, and any challenges encountered. This documentation serves as evidence of your hard work and provides a basis for presentations and publications. Develop clear and concise visual aids, such as charts, graphs, and slides, to effectively communicate your findings to others.

Participate in Competitions and Conferences

Competitions and conferences offer excellent platforms to keep you motivated with a deadline and gain visibility for your work.

Look for local, national, or international competitions and conferences that align with your field of interest. Submit your entry which could be art, writing, a research paper, or a project abstract to these events, highlighting your entry's significance and potential impact. Participating in such events not only provides exposure but also allows you to network with professionals and fellow researchers. Weight the return of investment and time it takes for every competition, and make a judgement. We cannot be part of all conferences and all competitions, but we can plan to pick the few that gives us the most motivation. Prize money from competitions can help us financially for colleges, so use that as a factor for prioritizing your entries as well.

Publish and Share Your Findings

Consider publishing your research findings or project outcomes in appropriate platforms such as scientific journals, online publications, social media, or even a personal blog. This not only contributes to the existing knowledge base but also establishes you as a credible researcher. Share your work on social media platforms, relevant forums, and communities to reach a wider audience and spark discussions around your research or project. Getting feedback from these forums helps you improve your initiatives.

Engage with the Media

Harness the power of the media to amplify your community service visibility. Write press releases or reach out to local newspapers, magazines, and online news outlets to share the purpose, mission, and expansion plan for your service. Emphasize the significance of your research, community service project, or organization that you built, and explain how it benefits society. Media coverage can generate public interest, attract potential collaborators, and increase your chances of expansion and grants including recognition.

Build an Online Presence

Create a professional online presence to showcase your work. Develop a personal website or portfolio that highlights your research or project, along with your achievements and accolades. Maintain an updated LinkedIn profile, and consider joining relevant online communities or forums to connect with like-minded individuals who are your supporters. Use your counselor's, parents' or other adults' help to monitor the activity on social media or if others contact you. This helps us use the social media for the right cause and be safe from online trolls and dangerous behaviors. As a high school student, we do not have the time and energy to do background checks on every individual, and this is where parents can help the most to protect us from any unwanted dangers.

Garnering Recognition

Garnering recognition as a student can be a rewarding experience that opens up opportunities for personal growth, leadership roles, and future endeavors. However, it's essential to approach recognition with integrity, responsibility, and dedication.

Here's a guide on how to gain recognition as a student and some potential challenges you may face:

Excel Academically

Strive to achieve excellence in your academic performance. Consistent high grades, involvement in challenging courses, and academic achievements can draw positive attention from teachers, peers, and college admissions committees.

Participate in Extracurricular Activities

Get involved in extracurricular activities that align with your interests and passions. Join clubs, sports teams, community service groups, or other organizations that showcase your talents and dedication.

Take Leadership Roles

Seek opportunities to take on leadership positions within your extracurricular activities. Leadership demonstrates initiative, responsibility, and the ability to guide and inspire others.

Contribute to Your Community

Engage in community service and volunteer work. Making a positive impact on your community reflects well on your character and commitment to the welfare of others.

Showcase Your Talents

Participate in competitions, performances, or exhibitions that showcase your talents, whether in academics, arts, sports, or any other area of expertise.

Develop Strong Interpersonal Skills

Cultivate effective communication and collaboration skills. Being able to work well with others and positively influence those around you will enhance your recognition.

Network and Build Relationships

Connect with teachers, mentors, and peers who can support and advocate for you. Building a strong network can open doors to recognition and opportunities.

Communicate Your Achievements

Don't be afraid to share your accomplishments modestly. Celebrate your achievements and let others know about your successes, but do so with humility.

Face Challenges with Resilience

Challenges are inevitable, and they may include competition, setbacks, or criticism. Approach challenges with resilience and a growth mindset. Learn from failures and use them as stepping stones to future success.

Avoid Seeking Recognition for the Wrong Reasons

Recognition should come from genuine effort and achievement, not from seeking attention or praise. Focus on making a meaningful impact rather than seeking external validation.

Challenges You May Face

Recognitions come with responsibilities. It may not be a smooth ride where everyone is inspired by you and are encouraging you. While most support, you will definitely have some challenges that you may have to deal with internally and externally.

Competition

Gaining recognition can be competitive, especially if you're in a high-achieving environment. Balancing your drive for recognition with healthy competition is crucial. Remember to be a good sport and have a healthy competition. You will come across students who are great peers and motivators. You will also find peers who are so competitive that it is unhealthy and unethical. Learn to find the difference and be kind to everyone, but stay away and have minimal contact with those unethical individuals if feasible. At the end of the day, we are all students who want to win, so you will find many characters just like the adults in our lives are exposed to at work.

Time Management

Juggling academics, extracurricular activities, and personal commitments can be challenging. Effective time management is vital to avoid burnout and maintain a balanced life.

Ethics and Integrity

Ethics is a big factor here for all students. It is important to avoid plagiarism, hiring researchers for your work, or making up details to get ahead under pressure of time to show for college admissions or other recognition. This will catch up with us, and internally, we are insulting our own ability. In the long run, this will lower our own self-esteem, even if nobody notices this, and we are wrongfully awarded for something we do not deserve. Remember that the college we go to is just 5 to 7percent of the years in our life. Is the admission that important that we are fine with losing our own self-esteem and the skill sets that make us unique?

Balancing Recognition and Humility

Strive for recognition without appearing arrogant. Cultivate humility, as it shows respect for others and a willingness to learn and grow. It is very easy to be egocentric, especially with so many things happening emotionally and psychologically in our brains. Be self-conscious, understand that you are not the only one who received the recognition—it is also the support system (that includes school, mentors, teachers, parents, and friends) who helped you get there. Ensure to give back your time and acknowledge the ecosystem who made who you are. For example: You will not be a Science fair winner if the local science fair and sponsoring organization did not put in the effort and your school did not help you. You may not be the scholarship winner if the teachers didn't spend their time writing that detailed recommendation.

Dealing with Rejection

Not every effort may lead to recognition, and facing rejection can be discouraging. Learn from disappointments and continue to pursue your goals. Personally, I have faced more rejections than recognitions, whether it was science fairs or competitions, but that has helped me move forward with a goal of wanting to improve.

Managing Expectations

Recognize that recognition may not always come instantly. Stay patient and committed to your journey, knowing that success often requires perseverance. Understand that awards and recognitions are motivators to keep the momentum and not an end result for your purpose.

Overcoming Imposter Syndrome

As you gain recognition, you may experience imposter syndrome, feeling like you don't deserve your achievements. Remember that recognition is a result of your hard work and dedication.

In conclusion, gaining recognition as a student involves a combination of academic excellence, involvement in extracurricular activities, leadership, community engagement, and strong interpersonal skills. Stay true to your values, face challenges with resilience, and remember that recognition is a byproduct of genuine effort, your support system that enabled you, and your dedication to your passions and goals.

Preparing for Prestigious Science Competitions and Scholarships

While I have mentioned the experience of science competitions, the same may apply to debates, traveling sports, Technology Student Association events, DECA, FBLA, 4-H, and many other events that I have not been part of. No matter the event or competition, enjoying the process and planning are crucial since many of these cannot be done beyond high school years.

Preparing for prestigious science competitions like the International Science and Engineering Fair (ISEF) or other similar challenges is an exhilarating and demanding journey that fosters innovation, critical thinking, and dedication among young researchers. For students eager to showcase their scientific prowess on an international stage, the preparation process is not just about winning accolades but about delving deep into the realm of scientific exploration.

To begin with, students aspiring to compete in ISEF or other challenges need to select a compelling research topic. The key to success lies in choosing an issue they are genuinely passionate about, as the road ahead will be filled with long hours of research and experimentation. The topic should be original, relevant, and address real-world problems to captivate the judges' attention. Once the subject is finalized, students must conduct an extensive literature review to understand the existing body of knowledge and identify any gaps in research that their project can address.

With the groundwork laid, the next step is to formulate a well-defined hypothesis and outline the experimental design. Precise planning and attention to detail are paramount, as this will serve as the blueprint for the entire project. Seeking guidance from mentors, teachers, or experts in the chosen field can be invaluable at this stage, providing insights and feedback that refine the project's direction.

Gathering the necessary resources and materials comes next, and this can be a challenge in itself. Securing lab equipment, chemicals, or any other essential components requires resourcefulness and networking. Many students often collaborate with universities, research institutions, or local industries to gain access to specialized equipment and expertise.

Once the experimentation phase commences, students must meticulously record their data and observations, maintaining a comprehensive lab notebook. This logbook not only helps keep the project stay organized but also serves as a crucial reference during the subsequent analysis and reporting stages.

The data analysis stage is where the project's significance and results start to take shape. Employing statistical tools and methods, students must critically analyze the data collected during the experiments to draw meaningful conclusions. The interpretation of results and pattern identification are essential aspects that contribute to the scientific merit of the project.

Simultaneously, young researchers must develop a captivating and concise presentation of their work. This includes creating an eye-catching poster, a well-structured research paper, and a compelling verbal pitch to communicate their findings effectively. Practice is key here, as refining the presentation takes time and effort.

With the project now complete, students often participate in local or regional science fairs to gain valuable feedback and exposure before the big event. These events serve as a dress rehearsal, allowing participants to fine-tune their presentations and address any potential questions or challenges raised by judges.

Aside from the scientific aspect, it's essential to consider the logistical side of participating in international events. Arranging travel and accommodations and navigating the logistics of transporting project materials can be daunting but necessary steps to ensure a smooth and rewarding experience. These usually happens in the months where students are preparing for AP exams and second term exams. Planning is very crucial for these exams; earlier and makeup dates need to be discussed with the schools.

Furthermore, participating in events like ISEF or other challenges provides an unparalleled opportunity for young researchers to interact with like-minded peers from around the globe. Networking with individuals who share a similar passion for science and innovation can lead to lasting friendships and potential future collaborations. The exposure to diverse perspectives and ideas fosters a broader understanding of global scientific issues and allows the chance to learn from the experiences of others.

As the event draws near, managing stress and nerves is important. The pressure to perform at an international level can be overwhelming, but you have to maintain a positive and focused mindset. Engaging in relaxation techniques, practicing mindfulness, and seeking support from friends and family can aid in keeping anxiety at bay. Additionally, rehearsing the presentation with peers, mentors, or in front of a mirror can enhance confidence and delivery.

During the event itself, participants should immerse themselves in the experience fully. Engaging with judges, attendees, and fellow participants helps create a lasting impression and opens doors for further collaboration and networking. It's essential to be receptive to feedback and take any criticism constructively, as it offers opportunities for improvement and growth.

Beyond the scientific presentations and competitions, ISEF and similar challenges often host a variety of workshops, seminars, college booths, and cultural events. Embracing these opportunities allows students to broaden their horizons, discover new fields of interest, and gain insights into different cultures. Being open-minded and inquisitive during these interactions can enrich the overall experience and leave participants with unforgettable memories.

After the event concludes, students have to take time for reflection. Celebrating their achievements and acknowledging the hard work put into the project is well-deserved. They should also assess their performance, highlighting areas of strength and areas that could be improved upon for future endeavors.

The benefits of participating in ISEF or other challenges extend well beyond the event itself. The experience of tackling a rigorous scientific project from start to finish builds valuable skills that will serve students well in their academic and professional pursuits. It demonstrates resilience, adaptability, and dedication—qualities that are highly valued in the scientific community and beyond.

Moreover, the recognition garnered through participation in prestigious science competitions can open doors for college admissions, scholarships, and research opportunities. Universities and institutions are often impressed by students who have showcased exceptional scientific aptitude and a commitment to innovation.

As participants return to their schools and communities, they become ambassadors of science, inspiring their peers to pursue scientific curiosity and exploration. Sharing their experiences and projects can ignite the spark of interest in other young minds, fostering a culture of scientific inquiry and problem-solving.

To continue building on their scientific journey, students can seek out mentorship and research opportunities, either through educational institutions or local research organizations. Many former ISEF participants have had the chance to work on groundbreaking projects with renowned scientists, leveraging their competition experience into a fruitful research career.

Preparing for ISEF or other challenges is a transformative process that demands dedication, passion, and a thirst for knowledge. Beyond the academic and personal growth, it provides a platform for young researchers to make a meaningful impact on the world through science. The experience of collaborating with peers, learning from experts, and presenting to a global audience is invaluable and sets the stage for future success in the scientific community. The journey may be challenging, but the rewards, both tangible and intangible, make it an experience of a lifetime. Through perseverance and a commitment to excellence, young scientists can make their mark on the world and pave the way for a brighter, more innovative future.

Understand the Competition

Familiarize yourself with the rules, guidelines, and judging criteria of ISEF. Study past projects and winners to gain insights into the types of projects that have been successful. Understand the categories and subcategories, and choose a project that aligns with your interests and expertise.

Select a Meaningful Project

Choose a project that is personally significant and addresses a problem or question you are genuinely passionate about. Look for opportunities to make a positive impact and contribute to your field of interest. Remember, the journey is just as important as the destination.

Conduct Thorough Research

Invest time in conducting extensive research on your topic. Review existing literature, scientific papers, and patents related to your project. Develop a deep understanding of the subject matter and identify knowledge gaps that your project aims to address. Collaborate with mentors, scientists, or experts in the field to gain valuable insights and guidance.

Plan and Execute Your Project

Develop a detailed project plan that includes timelines, milestones, and necessary resources. Break down your project into manageable tasks and allocate sufficient time for each step, including experimental design, data collection, analysis, and interpretation. Ensure that your methodology is robust and replicable.

Engage in Experimental Design

Carefully design your experiments, ensuring they are scientifically rigorous and address the research question or hypothesis. Pay attention to variables, controls, sample sizes, and statistical analyses. Seek guidance from mentors or advisors to validate your experimental design.

Collect and Analyze Data

Execute your experiments meticulously, collect accurate data, and maintain detailed records. Utilize appropriate data analysis techniques, such as statistical tests or data visualization, to draw meaningful conclusions. Seek feedback from experts in your field to validate your data analysis methods.

Communicate Your Findings

Develop effective communication skills to present your project. Create an engaging and visually appealing display board or poster that clearly conveys your research question, methodology, data, and conclusions. Practice delivering a concise and compelling oral presentation of your project to judges.

Embrace the Learning Process

While success in ISEF or other science challenges is a worthy goal, it is essential to embrace the learning process and personal growth that comes from participating in science fairs and challenges. Focus on expanding your knowledge, developing critical thinking skills, and refining your ability to communicate complex scientific concepts to a broader audience.

Seek Feedback and Improvement

Actively seek feedback from mentors, judges, and fellow participants. Embrace constructive criticism as an opportunity for growth and improvement. Incorporate suggestions and recommendations into your project, recognizing that iterative refinement is a valuable part of the scientific process.

Celebrate Personal Achievements

Recognize that success is not solely defined by winning a competition. Celebrate your personal achievements and the progress you've made throughout the process. Reflect on the skills, knowledge, and personal growth you have acquired, which will continue to serve you well beyond the science fair experience.

Emphasize Collaboration and Community

Science fairs and challenges provide an excellent opportunity to collaborate with peers, exchange ideas, and learn from each other. Engage in discussions, share insights, and support fellow participants. Embrace the sense of community that science fairs foster, knowing that collective learning and collaboration are essential for scientific progress.

Cultivate a Broader Perspective

While science fairs and challenges are valuable experiences, maintain a broader perspective on success. Recognize that science is a collaborative and iterative process that extends beyond competitions. Embrace failures and setbacks as opportunities for growth and discovery. Focus on the joy of exploration and the intrinsic value of scientific inquiry.

Preparing for these challenges requires careful planning, diligent research, and effective communication. While aiming for success is important, it is equally vital to view science fairs and challenges as opportunities for personal growth, learning, and contribution to the scientific community. Embrace the journey, learn from setbacks, and celebrate the knowledge and skills you acquire along the way. Remember, success is not solely determined by winning, but by the passion, curiosity, and perseverance you bring to your scientific endeavors.

Parent Note: In this process of achievement and visibility, there are several mundane, busy, and administrative tasks that you can discuss with your student and ask if they need help. It may be as simple as planning for printing, reminding them of their deadlines, ensuring food, clothes, and shoes are packed for the right activity or as simple as monitoring their emotions. At work, if a team is working towards a goal, we would help each other and ask your leader if you could help in any way for the team. Imagine our students as the leader for their high school years and offer help in a way that we are not overstepping their plans. Their usual answers may be "I know what I'm doing" or "No, I do not need help and can take care of it," but monitoring the threshold and ensuring they are safe, doing the right things even if it's the hard way, and being with them is very important. Siblings can also play a very important role here, no matter the age, where they can offer help if they are able to. This is a win-win since siblings can bond with each other and learn from each other.

LEADERSHIP

*"The beauty of empowering others is that your
own power is not diminished in the process."*

—ANDREW CARNEGIE

Description: *Contrary to popular belief, leadership doesn't always
mean being the president of every club at your school; it means instilling
and staying true to values and making sure to allow the participation
of others and equal perspectives when it comes to working in teams
and collaborating. In this chapter, we'll focus on how all of us can be
leaders and how that amplifies our application further.*

CHAPTER 13

Commitment and Leadership

Timing: Throughout high school years and beyond

High school serves as a crucial phase in a student's life, shaping their academic, personal, and professional journey. Preparing for college involves more than just academic achievements; it demands commitment and leadership to excel in various aspects of life. In this chapter, we will explore the significance of staying committed to oneself, contributing to the community, understanding that leadership extends beyond holding official titles, and creating recognition and visibility through dedicated commitment and effective leadership.

Staying Committed to Yourself

In the whirlwind of high school life, it is easy to lose sight of one's individual goals and aspirations. However, staying committed to oneself is essential for long-term success. Commitment to personal growth, passions, and dreams fosters resilience and determination. Students who dedicate themselves to self-improvement and stay true to their values stand out in college applications, demonstrating maturity and purpose. Moreover, colleges seek individuals who have a clear sense of direction and the dedication to pursue their chosen paths.

Helping Your Community

True leadership extends beyond individual accomplishments; it involves positively impacting the community around you. High school students can contribute to their communities through various initiatives, such as volunteering, organizing fundraisers, or participating in service projects. Demonstrating a commitment to giving back not only showcases empathy and compassion but also highlights an applicant's ability to work collaboratively and make a difference beyond personal interests.

Leadership Beyond Club Presidencies

Leadership roles in high school are often associated with being the president of a club or holding a prestigious position, but it can be demonstrated in everyday actions and behaviors. Students who take the initiative to mentor others, promote inclusivity, and inspire their peers exemplify true leadership qualities. Admissions officers appreciate students who show leadership potential in various ways, as it reflects their adaptability and versatility in different situations.

Creating Recognition and Visibility through Commitment and Leadership

Sustained commitment to a particular cause or interest can create recognition and visibility within the school and beyond. Whether it is excelling in academics, arts, sports, or community service, consistent dedication draws attention and admiration. Moreover, these achievements can be leveraged to showcase leadership skills when applying for college. Demonstrating that others look up to and rely on the student as a source of inspiration signifies a natural inclination towards leadership.

Balancing Commitment and Academic Excellence

While commitment and leadership are important, they should never come at the cost of academic excellence. High school students should strive for a balance between their extracurricular pursuits and their studies. Colleges seek well-rounded individuals who can manage their time effectively and excel in multiple areas. Demonstrating the ability to balance commitment and academic responsibilities portrays a student's organizational skills and time management abilities.

Challenges Faced and Lessons Learned

Commitment and leadership come with their fair share of challenges. High school students may encounter obstacles while juggling multiple responsibilities. However, these challenges provide valuable learning experiences. Admissions officers appreciate applicants who can reflect on their journey, acknowledge setbacks, and demonstrate resilience. Sharing stories of perseverance in the face of adversity showcases maturity and a growth-oriented mindset.

Empowering Others Through Leadership

One of the most powerful aspects of leadership in high school is the ability to empower others. True leaders understand that their role goes beyond personal achievements; it involves inspiring and uplifting their peers. By fostering a collaborative and supportive environment, student leaders can create a positive impact on the entire school community. This can be achieved through mentorship programs, workshops, or simply by being approachable and empathetic.

Leadership can manifest in unexpected ways, and it is often the little acts of kindness and encouragement that leave a lasting impression. A leader who takes the time to listen to others, offer help, and celebrate their successes is someone who inspires trust and respect. These qualities not only make a difference during high school but also set the foundation for future leadership roles in college and beyond.

Leading with Integrity and Ethics

As high school students prepare for college, it is crucial to understand that true leadership is rooted in integrity and ethics. Leaders who act with honesty, transparency, and fairness gain the trust of their peers and teachers alike. Admissions officers seek applicants who demonstrate strong moral principles and ethical decision-making. Leadership without integrity can be short-lived and may have negative consequences, undermining the leader's credibility.

Leading by example is a powerful way to instill ethical values in the school community. High school students who uphold a strong sense of integrity and treat others with respect create a culture of trust and unity. Such leaders are more likely to be recognized and respected by their peers, teachers, and college admissions committees.

Building Networks and Alliances

Commitment and leadership provide ample opportunities to build networks and alliances that can be valuable during the college application process and beyond. Engaging with teachers, mentors, and community leaders not only enhances personal growth but also opens doors to potential recommendation letters and opportunities for growth. Students should actively seek mentorship from teachers or professionals in their fields of interest. Mentorship can offer valuable guidance, personalized advice, and insights into potential career paths. Additionally, collaborating with like-minded peers on projects and initiatives fosters teamwork and strengthens interpersonal skills.

Overcoming Stereotypes and Perceptions

High school students aspiring to demonstrate commitment and leadership may encounter stereotypes and misconceptions about what it means to be a leader. Some may feel that leadership is reserved for the extroverted, outspoken individuals who hold official titles. However, in challenging these preconceptions, students can embrace their unique qualities. Introverted students, for example, can demonstrate leadership by leading through their actions, thoughtful decisions, and exceptional dedication to their pursuits. Emphasizing that leadership takes various forms and highlighting the unique contributions of each individual can lead to a more inclusive and supportive school environment.

Utilizing Technology for Impact

In the digital age, technology offers powerful tools for students to amplify their impact and reach a wider audience. Social media platforms, blogs, or websites can be utilized to showcase projects, community service activities, and initiatives, creating a portfolio of commitment and leadership efforts. This digital presence can enhance a student's visibility and recognition in college applications. While there's typically a stigma around how technology is used—more specifically towards how poorly it is used—it can definitely be used for positive benefit as well.

However, it is essential to use technology responsibly and mindfully. Oversharing or using social media irresponsibly can have adverse effects on a student's reputation. Students should be mindful of their digital footprint and use technology as a means to inspire, educate, and engage with their community positively.

Embracing Diversity and Inclusivity

Commitment and leadership in high school are also about fostering a culture of diversity and inclusivity. Embracing diversity means appreciating and respecting the differences among individuals in terms of background, culture, beliefs, and perspectives. Inclusive leadership means actively involving and valuing all members of the school community, ensuring that everyone feels heard, represented, and included.

Students can demonstrate their commitment to diversity and inclusivity by actively participating in clubs or organizations that promote cultural understanding, organizing events that celebrate various traditions, or initiating discussions about sensitive topics. By taking the lead in creating an inclusive environment, students not only contribute to the betterment of their high school but also exhibit qualities that colleges seek in prospective applicants.

Learning from Failures and Adaptability

Leadership and commitment are not immune to failures and setbacks. High school students should recognize that failure is a natural part of the learning process and an opportunity for growth. Admitting mistakes and learning from them showcases humility and resilience, qualities that are highly valued in college applicants. Adaptability is another crucial aspect of leadership. High school students should be open to change and willing to embrace new challenges. Adaptable leaders can navigate through uncertainties and effectively lead their peers, teams, or projects towards success.

Collaborative Leadership and Teamwork

While individual commitment and leadership are commendable, the ability to work collaboratively as part of a team is equally important. High school offers numerous opportunities to engage in group projects, sports teams, or extracurricular activities that require teamwork. Collaborative leaders inspire others, promote a sense of unity, and bring out the best in each team member. College admissions committees seek students who can thrive in diverse settings, cooperate with others, and contribute effectively to group dynamics. Demonstrating successful experiences as part of a team highlights the student's social and interpersonal skills.

Time Management and Prioritization

High school students preparing for college often find themselves with a wide array of commitments. Balancing academics, extracurricular activities, social life, and personal time can be challenging. Effective time management and prioritization are essential for maintaining commitment and leadership while excelling academically. Students can showcase their time management skills by outlining their involvement in multiple activities, sharing experiences of juggling responsibilities, and discussing how they achieved a healthy balance between their commitments.

The Long-Term Impact of High School Leadership

Commitment and leadership during high school extend beyond the college application process. The skills and experiences gained during these formative years can have a profound and lasting impact on a student's future endeavors. The dedication to causes and leadership experiences can shape career choices, personal values, and community engagement long after high school graduation. Moreover, high school leadership experiences often contribute to a student's personal growth and self-awareness. Through various challenges, successes, and failures, students develop a deeper understanding of their strengths, weaknesses, and passions.

Mentoring and Paying It Forward

As high school students grow into leaders, they have the opportunity to pay forward the support and mentorship they received. Becoming mentors to younger students or those in need can be a fulfilling way to make a positive impact on the next generation. Mentoring provides students with the chance to further develop their leadership skills, communication abilities, and empathy. It also demonstrates their commitment to giving back and supporting others in their pursuit of growth and success.

Commitment and leadership in high school are transformative experiences that shape a student's path to college and beyond. By staying committed to personal growth, helping their communities, embracing diverse perspectives, and leading with integrity, students can stand out as well-rounded and empathetic individuals in college applications.

Leadership extends beyond formal titles and involves empowering others, embracing failures, collaborating with teams, and effectively managing time. High school leadership experiences leave a lasting impact on a student's personal and professional development, influencing future decisions and career choices.

As students prepare to embark on their college journeys, they should reflect on the lessons learned from their commitment and leadership experiences in high school. By understanding the significance of these qualities and integrating them into their future endeavors, they can thrive not only in college but also in their roles as responsible, compassionate, and effective leaders in society.

CHAPTER 14

Navigating Applications and Acceptance into College

Timing: End of Junior and
Beginning of Senior Year

Navigating the College Application Process

Personally, the college application process was overwhelming for me. In the summer before senior year, I was part of a summer research program at MIT. I reached back home two days before my school started. As I entered my school doors for the senior year, I realized I was already behind with my essays and starting the Common App application process. It took me an entire weekend to organize myself to start on early action application vs regular applications. I went back and forth on the number of applications that I need to submit, the recommendation letters that I need to request and finally the number of essays I need to write along with my academic schedule and outside commitments. However, there were some principles that I decided to follow no matter the stress and the unknowns that were ahead of me.

Be Authentic in Your Application

When applying to colleges, be true to yourself in your application and apply in your terms, not what the admissions will look for. Showcase your genuine interests, experiences, and achievements. Admissions officers value authenticity and want to get to know the real you. Resist the temptation to exaggerate, embellish, or pretend to be someone you're not. From personal experience, my first version of the essay that I wrote was not myself. It was a bunch of words that did not portray me, and it did not answer the question they asked. When I re-read my essay carefully, it was all about external factors, and it was not who I was or want to be. Dig deep and question what you gained and lost in terms of personality after your four years in high school. What caused the changes?

Put yourself in the admission officers' shoes. They probably get two to three minutes to read your essay and all other parts of the application. They do not want the same generic story as everybody or, any hidden or subtle messages, where they need to figure out your strengths and weaknesses. How many essays do they read in a day? Is it fair to them if all we do is put together a jumble of extraordinary adjectives that we believe defines us? The truth is we all have imperfections, stories, and realizations in high school. Bring that out! No one expects us to be perfect human beings with great experiences where we never failed and learned. We all need not have heart-wrenching emotional stories. The truth is some of us are more privileged than many others with opportunities and support that not many have. If so, what did we do do with our opportunities and did we give back to others? Some of us may not be fortunate to grow with both parents in a household and the challenges are different from ours. Some of us have challenges being an athlete and that may have shaped us into the person we are. There are many unique stories and experiences that make us all different.

Choose Colleges That Align with Your Values

As you apply to colleges, consider institutions that align with your values and long-term goals. Seek out colleges that support your passions and offer programs that interest you. Applying to colleges that match your values will increase your chances of finding the right fit for your future. In the previous chapter on positive mindsets, I have a few factors that will help you decide on the universities you want to apply. A rule of thumb you will be given from your college counselor is to apply for three "Reach", three "Target", and four "Safety schools"—or something close to that. This depends on your finances and time. Understand the difference between "early action", "early decision", and "regular decision". Talk with your parents or guardians about financial stability and affordability. You do not want to apply for early decision, get accepted, not receive financial aid, and then find out that you cannot afford it. The time and effort will be wasted, not to mention there's an emotional toll of not being able to go to your first choice.

⚠️ Use collegvine.com or other similar websites to decide your Reach, Target and Safety schools. Your Reach schools are those dream schools where all of us want to be, but it may not be a reality to get a guaranteed acceptance. All Ivy leagues and Top 10 schools are a Reach for every student.

Your Target schools are those schools where your grades, scores, and portfolio fits well within their midrange.

Your Safety schools are those schools that you are 98% sure you will get accepted if you apply carefully following the instructions.

Understand your scores, classes, GPA, and extracurriculars, and create a free CollegeVine account to find your chances. This helps you get an understanding of the admission calculations. This may not be perfect, but will give you an idea.

Planning for Applications and Decisions

College application submissions are of several types to accommodate preferences and priorities of students. Familiarizing yourself with these application types, their impact on deadlines and the rules that govern them, is critically important.

The following table gives a high level overview of the types and how they can impact your priorities. Each college has its own process, hence I strongly suggest researching the type and the constraints provided by the college you are interested in.

	Early Decision (ED)	Early Action (EA)	Restrictive Early Action(REA)	Regular Decision	Rolling Admission
Process	Apply early	Apply early	Apply early	Apply by regular deadline date announced by the school	Apply throughout the admission cycle timeline
Decision	Receive decision early	Receive decision early	Receive decision early	Receive decision in spring of senior year	Receive decision based on when you applied
Commitment	Binding	Non-Binding	Non-Binding	Non-Binding	Non-Binding
Application to other schools	Cannot apply to other schools in early admission cycle	Can apply to other schools anytime	Can apply to other public schools early and any schools in Regular Decision timeline	Can apply to other schools simultaneously	Can apply to other schools

Plan with a Template:

Sample college planning template

1. List all the colleges with their deadlines (by early or regular), the number of recommendations needed, the essays needed apart from common app essay, portfolios needed, interview timings, financial aid deadlines, and decision dates.

2. Organize your files in either Google Drive or OneDrive by college. Have a document that states the college specific essays, deadlines, recommendations needed, scholarships, and financial aid for that college.

3. Create a resume, website, or LinkedIn profile by picking the most important activities and recognitions to you. There are many resume builder websites and LinkedIn provides help with creating a profile.

Portfolio/Resume sample

4. Start creating accounts in application portals, and fill in the known items that will not change before the application such as scores, address, parent details, your prioritized list of extracurriculars, subjects you took, awards, and other information.

5. Next plan your recommendations. Most of them request for one science or math, one humanities, and one additional recommendation. Create a recommendation template prep; a sample is below. Create this for every teacher you would like the recommendation from and narrow it down, so you can ask the teachers who you have the most positive points for.

Your recommendation request document can include questions as simple as below:

- List the subjects the teacher taught you in your high school years:

What were some of the topics, assignments, and team projects that you most enjoyed in this teacher's class?

- How is your relation with the teacher?

- Have you met this teacher outside the classroom, and does the teacher know you well?

- Is there any connection between the subject and topics taught in this class and what you plan to pursue in college?

- Did you have any challenges in this teacher's class that you discussed with the teacher, and did you overcome them?

- Could you provide any gentle reminders for the teacher on the work you did in the class that was a positive experience to emphasize and to include in your letter?

- Are there any other incidents where there was a personal connection with the teacher?

Once, you pick your recommenders, talk to your teacher face to face in a separate meeting thanking them for teaching you and send an email with your resume and prep document with the subject "Request for Recommendation—Your Name." Immediately send the recommendation request through Naviance, Common App, or any portal that the college requires. Some teachers provide several recommendations and having all of the information such as what you liked or did not like in their class, what were your learning moments and how this ties to your future aspirations, including your profile in one email is easier on them. Remember that teachers are doing you a favor, so be respectful to them and give them enough time before the to put this together.

Inform your guidance counselor on the universities you prioritized and the recommendations you requested. Create a recommendation prep document for your counselor as well. Provide your resume to your counselor too so they remember all the activities that you did in and out of the school. Counselors have to keep track of several students and their applications. The more information you provide them about your activities, likes, dislikes, passion, major you are planning to pursue, the better it is for them to ensure you are on track. Some schools request for this information in junior year, but provide this again to the counselor so they have the updates after your summer.

Sample Recommendation

Recommendation request sample email

Meet the counselor and ensure graduation requirements are met. Ensure all gaps such as documentation and signature on volunteer hours are taken care of well before deadlines. Review your transcript with the counselor for correctness, and if there are any mistakes, ensure they are fixed well in advance.

Ask if the counselor has time to review your application without the essays. This will help both the counselor and you to review for correctness and for the counselor to know what activities are important for you to be included in the counselor recommendation.

Finally, request for transcripts and their recommendation from the portal. These can all happen in one meeting or may happen in a set of meetings, but keep track of all the talking points needed and be prepared before the meetings. They have more work than you and you are not the only person in their mind, so being respectful of their time is very important. Help them if they request for time with other students and want you do some peer reviews.

Next, decide on your outside/other recommenders such as from your internships, research mentors, jobs, or other professional activities. Tailor the recommendation prep and resume to include information that may be valuable for the recommender outside your school and provide the details, if feasible, in a face-to-face meeting or zoom call. Mention the colleges you prioritized for applications and why. Another thing that may be helpful, if you have done several research or internships in your four years, is to take a general recommendation as soon as the internships or activity is complete. You can request for LinkedIn recommendations as well to make it easier on them and for you to be in touch.

Now comes the fun part! Essays—they are the most important thing, but they might be the most brain draining exercise that you will have to go through in all your years of school. You now have the job to package yourself and convince somebody that you have the skills and attitude to what it takes to be successful in a particular university. You *also* have the job to convince the audience to accept your application in few minutes. You *also* have to do a soul searching to understand yourself, which you might have never done before. You *also* have to explain the reasons behind why you did what you did in the last four years. You *also* have to show that you are good at what you do. You *also* have to show what you can do for the college and why you want to study there. You *also* have to show that you are more than your grades, scores, courses, and list of awards or activities.

This is not easy and it can come out as bragging or extremely modest, and both of these are not acceptable in this situation. A balance is needed, and we fear every word and sentence we write in that essay because of how admissions will read it.

Depending on your financial situation, there are private counselors or tutors who can guide you here if you have a writer's block.

Talk to your parents and request for help if you are stuck and do not know how to proceed here. There are local nonprofits and volunteers who are ready to help as well. Your mentors and teachers can guide you here.

However, you are responsible for it and anyone else writing for you can easily be seen through. Start simple by answering the question that the essays ask.

In my case, I started with college specific essays before I decided the common app personal statement. This was because I did not want to state the same thing multiple times, where the admission officer would be tired of reading the same narrative from me in multiple essays. I wanted every essay to show a different aspect of me and give more information rather than the same information as my activities, other essays, resume, and personal statement. Therefore, plan your essay topics for the colleges, write bullet points for each, cross check to ensure it is not the same information, and then elaborate.

Here are few tips that helped me:

- Be frugal with your words to start with.

- Start simple.

- Do not victimize yourself or give excuses in your essays.

- Do not load your essay with accomplishments and awards that are in the activity section.

- Confirm you answered the essay question asked.

- Confirm if you are talking about you or if you are talking about someone or something else in the essay. This is a common mistake students make. They forget what is needed to convey the message and share some irrelevant details which may be not required.

- If the essay is about an event that made you realize something, show the event. If it's about your extra-curricular, show your passion and purpose.

- In short-answers, be truthful. Do not write responses to impress someone.

- Share with an adult who does not know you well, but is still trusted, and ask them to confirm if you answered the essay topic and provide for open feedback. This is the most helpful way to ensure a person who does not know you understood who you are. I found that I would miss details in my essays because I assumed details are not needed with the word count I had. However, a more distant person reading it wants to know the detail behind what happened and why to understand us better.

- Start early on the essays and do not write it in a day. I started in August and took until the last day to re-read it multiple times and make edits.

- I requested my parents to condense my essay writing during our Labor Day weekend vacation trip, where I could write it away from my desk and academic work. My parents ensured I had the space and were fine if I didn't participate in the daily hiking planned. Authors and writers do this often, and having published a book before, I knew that doing it in the same daily surroundings makes it tough for me to focus and write. This helped me focus on understanding myself. Retrospectively, I have great memories on how and where I wrote my essays. This may be different for you. You may have a favorite corner in your home or library and can plan for that.

Here are some of my sample essays. I am unsure how my essays came across to its readers or to you, when you read them, but it came from experiences unique to me and my thoughts.

Prompt: Talk about a time when you had an accomplishment, event, or realization that sparked a period of personal growth and a new understanding of yourself or others.

It's February 2020. I shuffle into my seat as the man in front of me slowly opens his binder and smiles as he looks straight into the camera. I had just won a national science contest for developing a prototype for early diagnosis of opioid addiction, and I had a series of press interviews lined up by the organizers. It was my 3rd media interview of the day; I was enjoying the attention and was excited to talk about my work.

A few minutes into the interview, I heard the question. "A 14-year-old girl shouldn't wear a business coat; why don't you dress your age?" I was taken aback. I had heard a variant asked a few times, but it always felt wrong. It wasn't about the dress at all. It was all about my age, and the implication was that I was too young to talk about serious science.

As usual, I simply smiled and said, "I don't know." Even though I put on a brave front, it was very painful to hear. Is this really how people viewed me? Was what I wore more important than what I said? What about my work?

At first, I didn't quite understand why some would question my maturity in dealing with big social problems. Some others would try to "simplify" my work assuming real solutions are beyond me. Maybe it was my science or a lack of rigor in my research. It took me a while to realize that my presence, a short, high school sophomore girl talking about research in advanced topics, somehow came across as foreign to many in the science community. Most assumed I was not competent to understand the subject, and sometimes even my research and conclusions were suspected. It was hurtful, to say the least. Nobody wanted me in the one place I wanted to be.

My excitement and spirit, which once came naturally, were consistently hampered by external opinions and expectations rather than my own. My confidence slumped. I stopped doing new research as I feared ridicule and kept talking about old work, seeming to crave validation. I felt nobody could challenge me or find faults if I didn't discuss new subject areas. I lost the sense of fearlessness I once had of wading into new areas.

Then unexpectedly, one day, I got a note from my mentor, who had been observing my work all along. She said something that resonates with me till today. "Be cautious of recognition. Not everybody applauds your scientific achievement; they applaud the effort of a 15-year-old regardless of the results. Don't lose your sense of purpose and keep working hard" She spoke from her experience as an acclaimed scientist and had been through what I was going through. The more I spoke about it with her, I felt like someone understood my insecurities. Amongst the noise, a sane voice of encouragement helped me find my joy and purpose in building things and solving problems.

I decided to double down on my convictions and things that made me naturally happy. It wasn't easy, but very exciting to screen out what others think and do whatever makes me happy. It took me some time, but eventually, I found myself exploring new ideas, playing and learning new concepts, and synthesizing new solutions. I focused on fearlessly expanding my work's horizons and sharing it with passion. Maybe I didn't dress my age, but the work that I was doing wasn't "my age" either. I was a young girl spending whatever time I could muster working in a lab and developing solutions for metallic contamina-

tion of water, opioid addiction, and cyberbullying. What truly mattered was my work and my drive, which continues today.

While a simple smile was a fitting response to the interviewer's question then, today, I am convinced that there is much more to me than my outfit.

An essay on one of my extracurriculars that gives me pleasure:

The wind picks up as I try to land from 8000 feet over Boulder, CO, but a slight drift knocks me off course, and I almost miss the runway. I correct the ailerons of my glider and land right in the middle.

Since my solo that late summer day in 2021, I have piloted a glider several times and am weeks away from my license.

Considering the pressures of school and other activities, I enjoy the quiet freedom of open skies. I often find myself with just airplane instruments, soaring with wind currents, admiring the beauty of mountain peaks. Always humbled by the majesty of nature, I return re-energized for the next challenge.

I plan to continue this passion in the future, flying more complex planes and traveling further. Out there is a beautiful world, and I want to experience more of it—10,000 feet above the ground.

Essay sharing my experiences and how I think of myself:

When Marshall McLuhan said, "There are no passengers on spaceship earth; we are all crew," he might as well be talking about my life which I see as a consequence of the actions of many who shaped me into the person I'm today. Being of multicultural ethnicity and exposed to the world through my innovation workshops in schools globally, I've grown to see myself learning from my "Kathak" dance partners in Denver, Arab girls in Riyadh, and fellow BTS fans in Seoul. I have attended 7 different schools since the age of 4. I have traveled to 25 countries for my innovation workshops and learned to appreciate the art, culture, and diversity of thought. My parents encouraged trying new things, even risking failure.

Growing up, I was fortunate that my parents met my basic needs. My father says, "Those who have more need to give more." I feel a tremendous responsibility to give back to my community by introducing the power of STEM education. Being part of the Children's Kindness Network organization taught me that empathy and kindness are the prerequisites to solving any problem in our community. It drives all my work developing solutions to social and environmental problems and my aspiration to continue research in areas of cell biology. Solving big community problems should be my generation's responsibility, and I try to contribute as much as possible.

I am proud of my heritage, which encourages exploration and social responsibility, and grateful to my community for their support.

Portfolio and Videos

Some universities ask for optional portfolios or videos to showcase your work beyond your normal application. Take advantage of that. You can share your research, art, music, writing samples, products, and more. Create this far in advance of the deadline. Portfolio submissions usually have a few extra days than the required application. This was not very clear when I started my application process. For some colleges, you can start your portfolio submission in a separate portal, and for some colleges, you apply and then you will get a link to submit your portfolio. You can find it easily from their websites. Don't make it optional if you have something else to share. This is a chance to show your personality, your face, your confidence, and your passion in a format where they can see you in action.

Know the scholarship deadlines for these colleges and apply to them earlier. Once you apply, wait for the interviews, if applicable. Be prompt in responding to your interviewers. Be on time for the interview, be cordial, and answer any questions they may have on your activities and academics and why you want to attend their specific university. Interviewers are alumni, so you can ask them questions about the universities, what they liked, and what they didn't like about attending there.

Here are few general guidelines to prepare for the interviews:

Monitor your email closely after you applied for the schools. If you receive the interview request, promptly respond with several schedule options to the interviewer. If feasible, pick a time where you can reach earlier, can spend more than the allotted 45 minutes and do not have homework deadlines looming over your head. Study your application and be ready with at least 2-3 questions for the interviewer. If you applied to your dream school, I am sure you will have questions on what, why and how you will want to spend time in the school for the next 4 years. You may have questions on why they chose the school, what they liked about it or what they disliked about it, the major the interviewer chose, and the final career path they are in today. Interviewers are alumni for those schools and are volunteering their time for us. Respect their time and make it valuable for them.

Next, ensure to prepare a concise answer for the following general questions:

1. Tell me about yourself. Be concise providing an update on who you are, which school you go to, what are your passions and what you are hoping to study and your potential long term career. I personally do not believe accomplishments and awards define you. They are just a reward for the passion you followed.

2. What are you hoping for from the University you applied to? Share what you plan to do there such as pursue a major, but potentially explore a minor, pre-professional clubs that you may be interested in, and other things that you had planned to.

3. What extracurricular activities are you involved in or based on the response to your first question, to elaborate more on your passion? Get into a detail on why you started what you started, when did you start and how long you were committed to this, why you love it and future plans to continue in and out of your accepted college.

4. What are your strengths and weakness? In my opinion, the skills mentioned in this book should not be your strengths or weakness—such as time management, teamwork, collaboration, communication, positive mindset, planning are essential skills to survive in college. We have learned and improved these in the last 4 years and hence you are here for an interview, so bringing these up shows that we are very pointed and focused on the portfolio. I would focus on something else such as a talent, your ability to doodle or draw mindmaps for taking notes as a strength, inability to cook as a weakness, your fashion sense, your musi-

cal ability, your courage to speak up, being an introvert or extrovert, or some other activity or qualities that is part of your life. This need not be necessary for surviving day to day. This will show you are more than your portfolio and academics.

5. Finally be ready to share your favorite subject, your creative skills and why you believe the school is your dream school and why you want to be badly there.

The day of the interview, ensure to be early to your interview venue—in person or remote. If it's a public space such as a cafe or a restaurant, settle down before the interviewer reaches there and get water or a drink. Interviewers usually do not want to bring a resume or our portfolio. Unless they mentioned, do not carry it. I always a carried a pen and notepad to take notes on their answers so I can look back. Be presentable no matter the time of the day. Greet your interviewer, be cordial and open up the discussion. All the interviewers I had were very courteous and made me feel comfortable as the discussion continued. There may be a moment of silence in the beginning, but confirm if you answered their questions if there is an uncomfortable silence. This will help them asking more clarifications. Be humble no matter your accomplishments and awards. Ask your questions when they are ready. If you find something else interesting about the interviewer, ask them about it. One of my interviewers introduced herself and mentioned she changed majors midway and I was curious to know why she took that path. I always ended the interview with asking them if they wanted to know anything else about me to ensure both sides are clear on learning about each other.

Wait for a decision. Some colleges will send you letters requesting for more information, so be prompt and respond. At this point, you do not have any more control over your decisions; the only control you have is to finish the semester and year strong. Enjoy your last few months in high school, commit more time to your activities, and plan to sustain your organization or activity beyond your schedule. Find a way to recruit more volunteers, and create a process to self-sustain. Thank your teachers, counselor, interviewers and mentors for all their help. Search for scholarships that you can still apply for and find a way to pay for your education as much as you can.

Remember That Rejections Happen

Receiving an early rejection letter from your early decisions or early action college can be disheartening, but it's essential not to take it personally. College admissions are competitive, and rejections are a part of the process. Understand that rejection doesn't define your worth or potential. Stay resilient, and know that the right college for you is out there.

Research other colleges, visit their campuses if you can, and see what they offer. You want to find a place where you'll be happy and thrive.

When you see others succeeding or getting accepted, celebrate their accomplishments genuinely and use their achievements as inspiration to push yourself further. Instead of feeling envious or inadequate, focus on your unique talents and strengths. Your journey is not a race against others; it's a personal exploration of your potential. Be proud of who you are and what you've accomplished, regardless of the outcome.

Remember that rejection is a natural part of the college application process. If you encounter disappointment, view it as an opportunity to grow, learn, and explore different paths. The right college fit for you will recognize your authenticity and value your contributions.

In the end, staying true to yourself is about honoring your values, passions, and dreams. It's about acknowledging your worth and refusing to compromise your identity to fit societal expectations or peer pressures. Embrace your individuality—it will make you stand out the most in your college application process.

Summary

As you navigate high school and the college application process, keep in mind that staying true to yourself is a lifelong journey. It will continue to shape your choices and decisions beyond high school and college. Embrace challenges, cherish achievements, and remain committed to living an authentic life that aligns with your deepest values.

In a world where comparison and conformity can be all too tempting, remember that your uniqueness is your greatest asset. Stay true to yourself, and you will not only thrive in high school and college but also have a fulfilling life with purpose and meaning. So, go forth with confidence, unafraid to shine as the true and remarkable individual that you are!

For many of the students who are curious of my acceptances, I got accepted into Harvard, Stanford, MIT, Yale, Duke and couple others I applied to. I knew fairly well what I wanted to do in each of these schools if I were to choose any of them.

It was a tough decision for me because any of these prestigious schools could have been my home for the next four years. For me, continuing my responsibility of advocating for an innovation curriculum, providing equitable resources for education, building a strong foundation of academic knowledge, and research in my areas of interest were the decision factors. The final decision came to potential research opportunities and being close to my mentors who believed in me supported me throughout high school. I am confident each one of you will have a list of your own college list acceptances and your own dream halls you want to walk in.

CHAPTER 15

Celebrating Success and Dealing with Recognition

Timing: Throughout high school years and beyond

Celebrate success, don't let it get to your head, and look forward!

Success is a significant boost of confidence in a student's journey through school. Whether it be acing an exam, securing a dream job, or achieving a personal goal. Celebrating these accomplishments is vital for self-validation and motivation. However, as we bask in the glory of success, there is a fine line between embracing achievement and letting it foster arrogance or complacency. This chapter delves into the art of celebrating success while maintaining humility and staying driven to reach new heights.

Acknowledge the Journey

To celebrate success while maintaining humility, recognize the efforts and dedication invested in reaching the milestone. Success is seldom an overnight achievement; it is the culmination of perseverance, hard work, and sacrifices. By acknowledging the journey, one remains grounded and appreciative of the process that led to the triumph.

When reveling in success, take time to reflect on the obstacles faced and the lessons learned along the way. Appreciating the growth and personal development that transpired throughout the pursuit of success fosters a humble mindset. It reminds us that there is always more to learn, and each achievement is a stepping stone towards greater excellence.

Gratitude and Humility

Expressing gratitude for success and acknowledging the support of others is a key aspect of celebrating triumph with humility. Success is seldom a solitary endeavor, and recognizing the contributions of mentors, friends, family, and colleagues reinforces the importance of collective effort. A humble attitude is not only appreciative of others' support but also genuinely celebrates their achievements. Instead of competing or comparing, embrace a collaborative mindset that celebrates the successes of others as much as your own. This fosters a positive and encouraging environment where everyone thrives. Moreover, success should not be used as a means to elevate oneself above others. Maintain humility by avoiding boastful behavior and arrogance. Recognize that there will always be more to learn, and every achievement is an opportunity for growth, rather than a reason to feel superior.

Embrace Continuous Improvement

As we celebrate success, it is essential to understand that it should not mark the end of our journey, but rather a milestone on a continuous path of improvement. Complacency is the nemesis of progress, and allowing success to get to our heads may hinder future growth. The key to avoiding complacency is to set new goals and objectives after each achievement.

Celebrate the success briefly, but quickly redirect focus to the next challenge. Embrace a growth mindset, viewing success not as the pinnacle of achievement but as a springboard for greater endeavors.

Create a roadmap for the future, outlining short-term and long-term objectives. Establish specific, measurable, achievable, relevant, and time-bound (SMART) goals that push your boundaries and encourage constant growth. By channeling your energy into continuous improvement, you remain humble and hungry for more achievements.

Stay Humble Through Failures

In the pursuit of success, failures are inevitable. However, how we handle setbacks defines our character and our ability to stay humble. Understand that failures are opportunities to learn, grow, and strengthen our resolve.

Avoid letting failure deter you from your aspirations. Rather, embrace it as a part of the journey and a chance to refine your approach. Approach failures with a growth mindset, seeking to identify the lessons they hold and incorporating them into your future endeavors. Furthermore, staying humble through failures requires accepting responsibility for mistakes and learning from them. Resist the urge to blame external factors or other individuals, but instead, focus on self-improvement and resilience.

Personally, I have learned a lot when I failed. When I started my first book proposal, I had about 28 publishers who rejected before somebody decided to trust me. Similarly I had many failures with scholarships, science fair projects, and I even struggled in some courses. However, I think I learnt from them and tried to better the next time.

Seek Constructive Feedback

To avoid succumbing to overconfidence, actively seek constructive feedback from mentors, peers, and supervisors. Welcoming feedback demonstrates a willingness to learn and improve, indicating humility in the face of success. Remember, "Feedback is a Gift". You should accept it and cherish it.

When receiving feedback, approach it with an open mind and without defensiveness. Constructive criticism offers valuable insights that can lead to further growth and development. Embrace feedback as an opportunity to refine your skills and enhance your future performance. Moreover, encourage a culture of feedback within your personal and professional circles. Be receptive to providing feedback to others, supporting their growth as they support yours. By fostering a feedback-oriented environment, you create a supportive network that values continuous improvement and keeps success in perspective.

Engage in Mentorship and Coaching

Mentorship and coaching play integral roles in personal and professional development. Engaging with mentors who have experienced success and humility can provide invaluable guidance. They can offer insights on how to maintain a balanced perspective amid achievements and challenges. Mentors and coaches can also help set realistic expectations and identify areas for improvement. They serve as a source of motivation, reminding you of the bigger picture and your long-term objectives.

By seeking mentorship, you actively demonstrate your commitment to growth and humility. Embrace their guidance and remain open to their advice, for they have navigated similar paths and understand the importance of staying grounded.

During self-reflection, assess your actions, thoughts, and emotions. Are you maintaining a humble and growth-oriented mindset? Are you treating others with respect and kindness, regardless of their achievements? Identifying areas for improvement allows you to make conscious efforts to remain grounded.

Additionally, practice gratitude daily. Be grateful for the opportunities and support that contributed to your success. Gratitude helps reinforce humility by reminding you of the interconnectedness of achievements and the impact of others on your journey.

In the pursuit of success, it is essential to find a delicate balance between celebrating achievements and remaining humble. By acknowledging the journey, expressing gratitude, embracing continuous improvement, learning from failures, seeking constructive feedback, engaging in mentorship, and practicing mindfulness, you can celebrate success without succumbing to arrogance or complacency. Striving for the next checkpoint with humility and determination ensures that success becomes a catalyst for future growth and an opportunity to make a lasting, positive impact on yourself and those around you.

Reacting After Receiving the Decision of Your First College (Whether It's Your Top Choice or Not)

Receiving the decision of your first college, regardless of whether it's your top choice or not, can evoke a range of emotions and require thoughtful consideration of your next steps. Here are some suggestions on how to react and navigate the situation:

Give Yourself Time to Process

It's completely normal to experience a mix of emotions upon receiving a college decision. Whether you receive an acceptance, rejection, or waitlist notification, allow yourself some time to process your feelings. Take a deep breath, acknowledge your emotions, and remind yourself that this is just one step in your journey.

Celebrate Your Achievements

If you receive an acceptance letter or sometimes a rare likely letter, take a moment to celebrate your accomplishments. Receiving an offer from one of the colleges of your choice is a significant achievement and a testament to your hard work and dedication. Share the news with your loved ones, take pride in your accomplishments, and allow yourself to revel in the excitement.

Reflect on Your Options

After receiving a decision, take the time to reflect on your options. If the college is your top choice and you were accepted, that's fantastic! Consider what factors contributed to your decision, such as the academic program, campus culture, location, or financial aid package. If you were not accepted to your top choice, remember that there are plenty of other excellent colleges and universities that could be a great fit for you. Take the opportunity to reassess your priorities and evaluate the other options available to you.

Weigh Your Alternatives

Even if you received an acceptance from your top choice, it's essential to carefully consider your other options. Review the acceptance letters from the other colleges you applied to, and compare them in terms of academics, extracurricular opportunities, financial aid, location, and other factors that are important to you. Keep an open mind and objectively evaluate each option.

Seek Guidance and Support

Reach out to your school counselor, teachers, or mentors for guidance and support. They can provide valuable insights and help you make sense of the decision. Discuss your options with your trusted confidants and listen to their perspectives. Ultimately, the decision is yours, but it can be helpful to gather input from those who know you well and have your best interests at heart.

Consider Visiting or Researching Colleges

If you haven't already visited the colleges on your list, consider scheduling visits or virtual tours to gain a better understanding of the campuses, facilities, and student life. Additionally, conduct thorough research on each institution, exploring their academic programs, resources, extracurricular activities, and alumni success stories. This information will aid in making an informed decision.

Evaluate Financial Aid Packages

Review the financial aid packages offered by each college. Take into account tuition costs, scholarships, grants, and potential loan amounts. Consider the long-term financial implications and how they align with your future goals. If necessary, reach out to the financial aid offices for clarification or to discuss any concerns.

Keep an Open Mind

Remember that college decisions are not a reflection of your worth or potential. Admissions processes can be highly competitive, and many factors influence the outcome. Keep an open mind and embrace the possibilities that lie ahead. The college you choose will provide unique opportunities for growth, learning, and personal development.

Stay Positive and Focused

Regardless of the decision you received, maintain a positive mindset and remain focused on your goals. Use the news as motivation to continue working hard academically and engaging in meaningful extracurricular activities. Your college experience is what you make of it, and success can be achieved at any institution with dedication and perseverance.

Move Forward Confidently

Once you have evaluated your options and made a decision, embrace it wholeheartedly. Trust in your judgment and be confident in the path you have chosen. Remember that your college experience is just the beginning of a lifelong journey of learning and growth.

In conclusion, reacting to the decision of your first college requires a combination of reflection, evaluation, and careful consideration. Embrace the emotions, seek guidance when needed, and make a decision that aligns with your goals and aspirations. Keep a positive mindset, and remember that no matter which college you choose, your dedication and commitment will play a significant role in shaping your future success.

CONCLUSION

As I conclude this book and my thoughts, I wanted to share that your journey may be very different than mine. What we cannot change in the college application process is our economic background, the family we are born in, our parents' education and work, the high school we went to, or our location, since these were decided for us. However, what we can control is our character, our responsibility, our passion for a cause, our course plans, our relationships, our networks, and our attitude. While many students want to be in the top selective college campus, we cannot control the decisions we get, but we can influence how we craft our applications. Colleges are trying to get the best candidates that have a diverse perspective to make up a class and we are trying to get in to the right one where we may thrive.

The general rule I followed was that I will aim for the best where I believe I will thrive, but I will have alternative ones with a priority list, which will still shape me into a person I want to be. Yes, location does matter, but I will be flexible and adaptable. Yes, peers matter, but we do not get to select peers all the time. Yes, climate and weather matters, but there are many colleges in the same vicinity that will give me the same experience. Yes, ranking matters, but not if I find other opportunities. Yes, a great dorm matters, but I will manage for a few years. I could not get all that I wanted, so I decided on the top three factors that would make or break my college experience, and I was ready to be flexible with the other factors.

No matter what, I was confident that I used my high school years to develop skills such as communication, speech, writing, and study habits that fit me. I collected a wealth of experiences that were memorable and made a lot of friends in and outside school that I can lean on.

THANK YOU AND NEXT STEPS

Hopefully, you were able to gain a better understanding of what high school should truly consist of and a little bit about how the college admissions process is what *you* make it to be. As I'm writing and wrapping up this book, I'm actively packing for college, ready to take my next steps. I hope one day all of you can be equally excited to go to college as I am.

Your journey is your own, so don't let anybody stop you and hinder your abilities to change the world and make high school exactly what you want it to be.

So all the best, keep your head up, stay positive, take those risks, and look for the good, but don't ignore the bad. I hope you enjoy your journey as much as I did!

Signing off, until next time!

Acknowledgments

Writing this book *Young Innovator's Guide to Planning for Success* was a labor of love to put on paper my experiences so that others can benefit from my experiences in my high school years. The writing journey brought back memories of all individuals who saw some promise in me, nurtured my passion, and guided me through a path to where I stand.

My teachers from STEM School Highlands Ranch ignited my thirst for knowledge, while sometimes preparing me for a self-reliant future. My principal Mr. Ryan Alsup, former Executive director Penny Eucker, and college counseling team led by Ms. Kelly Myrick, meticulously helped me chart my academic course, giving me room to pursue my passions. Their unwavering belief in my potential became the very foundation of this book.

My immense gratitude to mentors who played pivotal roles in my development beyond the walls of the school. Dr. Pardis Sabeti, whose pioneering work in infectious diseases continues to inspire young minds like mine, offered invaluable insights into the world of research and the courage to challenge existing paradigms. Dr. Sangeeta Bhatia's infectious enthusiasm for bioengineering and her dedication to bridging the gap between science and medicine instilled in me the importance of human-centered innovation. Mr. Selim Tezel, from the MIT App Inventor team continues to be a huge pillar of support. Finally, Dr. Michael McMurray, whose guidance and mentorship down the years, especially during moments of self-doubt in my research, reminded me that every misstep is a chance to recalibrate and grow.

Thanks to my parents and grandparents, who navigated the ups and downs with me. Your belief and advocacy, even when I doubted myself and was ready to quit, was the anchor that kept me grounded and humble. Thanks to my younger brother, Anirudh, who sometimes missed his activities to help me finish my work. Our collective laughter growing up together reminded me that my greatest aspirations began with a simple shared joy with my loved ones.

This dedication extends to all my friends, classmates, college advisors, to the students in the Kakuma refugee camps, the students and educators who I met during my innovation workshops, who all offered a helping hand or a listening ear. Their non-stop dedication to improve themselves inspired me to keep going.

Finally, to the young dreamers and changemakers who hold this book in their hands: never underestimate the power of your curious minds. Let this guide be a recipe, which you build on as you forge your own unique path. Dream boldly, fail bravely, and most importantly, never lose sight of the spark that ignites your passion. As you navigate the twists and turns of your high school years, remember— every one of you has the potential to change the world no matter where you end up for your undergraduate studies.

With deep gratitude,
Gitanjali Rao

About the Author

Gitanjali Rao is an inventor, aspiring scientist, author, speaker, and active worldwide promoter for STEM. She was recognized as America's Top Young Scientist and received a President's Environmental Youth Award (PEYA) from the Environmental Protection Agency (EPA) for her patented invention of a lead contamination detection tool. Gitanjali is also the inventor of Epione, a device for early diagnosis of prescription opioid addiction through genetic engineering, and Kindly, an anti-cyberbullying service that uses AI and Natural Language processing.

She was honored in *Forbes* "30 Under 30 in Science" in 2019 and as *TIME*'s "Top Young Innovator" and "Kid of the Year" for her innovations and STEM workshops she conducts globally, which has inspired over 75,000 students across six continents and forty-five countries in the last three years.

In 2021, she was appointed a UNICEF Youth Advocate because of her work in using science to solve social problems such as cyberbullying and developing solutions for environmental protection. She recently received a Muhammad Ali Humanitarian Award for her selfless service for the Kakuma refugee camp students in Kenya.

She will be attending Massachusetts Institute of Technology starting in fall 2023.